Evelyn Jacks

ESSENTIAL TAX FACTS

*Simple Ways to Put More Money in Your
Pocket at Tax Time and All Year Long*

KNOWLEDGE BUREAU
NEWSBOOKS

WINNIPEG, MANITOBA, CANADA

ISBN No. 1-897051-25-5

Printed and bound in Canada

Canadian Cataloguing in Publication Data

Jacks, Evelyn 1955-

Evelyn Jacks essential tax facts: simple ways to put more money in your pocket at tax time and all year long –2005 ed.

Includes Index
ISBN No. 1-897051-25-5

1. Income tax –Canada – Popular works. 2. Tax planning – Canada – Popular works. I. Title. II. Title: Essential tax facts

HJ4661.3212 2005   343.7105's   C2005-900153-4

Published by:
Knowledge Bureau, Inc.
Box 52042 Niakwa Postal Outlet, Winnipeg, Manitoba R2M 0Z0
204-953-4769 Email: reception@knowledgebureau.com

Research Assistance: Walter Harder and Associates

Editorial Assistance: Cordell Jacks, Elisabeth Schimke

Cover and Page Design: Frank Reimer

CONTENTS

Introduction

Chapter 1 Essential Tax Facts for Individuals and Families

Why do Canadians pay too much tax? There are double-digit reasons why you should care to gain control of your after-tax dollars. A few simple tax facts can get your started:

Chapter 2 Essential Tax Facts for Employees

A cornerstone of sound tax reduction strategies is to "pay yourself first". . . especially if you are an employee. To create real wealth within your employment scenario, it also helps to tap into equity. That's why you should:

Chapter 3 Essential Tax Facts for New Investors

So you want to be a millionaire? Then get a grip on your largest lifetime expense—your taxes—and start earning tax efficient investment income with the help of simple tax facts:

Chapter 4 Essential Tax Facts for Wealth Preservation

Savvy management of time and money results in powerful productivity. The tax system can really help, especially if you face funding both the university-bound and your own retirement at mid life.

Chapter 5 Essential Tax Facts for The Self Employed

Making the break to the freedom of self-employment? Get organized for a new relationship with CRA and take charge of your after tax cash flow. Here are the facts you need to know:

Chapter 6 Essential Tax Facts for Singles and Seniors

When you think about it, the young and the old often have so much in common—they are often in transition to or from conjugal relationships, jobs, cities, homes. Yet they are often also primary caregivers to others. Special attention should be conferred upon:

ESSENTIAL TAX FACT SHEETS

Money Saving Tax Tips at a Glance

The following Essential Tax Fact Sheets contain time-dated detailed tax filing information that changes with budgets and indexing. This information is provided to you at no extra charge on The Knowledge Bureau website. It is provided to supplement your reading of this book, drill down on tax tips you may require to file your return or ask better questions of your advisors. It will also enhance the value of your investment in this book by keeping you current with ongoing tax change. To access this information, simply go to www.knowledgebureau.com and click on the icon that represents the cover of this book. For those who wish to receive hard copy, please call us toll free: 1-866-953-4769. Please quote the ISBN no. on the backcover.

INTRODUCTION

Did you know that the biggest expense in your lifetime will be your tax bill?

That's right, for most people it's higher than their mortgage, car or kids' education. Most Canadians go to work every day for almost half the year just to pay their taxes! You really don't start working for yourself until sometime in the late spring, depending on where you live in Canada.

Further, the decisions you make about how and where you work and invest, the resulting amount of taxes you pay, income you keep and capital assets you accumulate, will be most greatly influenced over the long run by your knowledge of tax reducing strategies.

In short, it's not just about filing a tax return on time, it's about taking control of how much tax you pay throughout your lifetime, and making sure you pay only the correct amount and not one cent more!

When you think about your taxes as a lifetime commitment, the numbers are too large to ignore. For example, the average annual tax bill for most Canadians is just over $8000. Multiply that by a 40 year working life and you'll pay over $300,000! Imagine shaving just 10%, 15% or 20% off that large figure each and every year. . . you could add $30,000 to $60,000 to your retirement, home ownership or educational savings plans very easily!

Got your interest?

When it comes to tax planning, so many average Canadians tune out, thinking "that's for the rich!" Not so. You can't afford not to take control.

Tax reduction strategies are especially important for average Canadians who go to work day in and day out and struggle with too much debt and too little time to manage their affairs wisely. In fact, most low income families actually pay a higher marginal rate of taxes than our richest citizens. . .because of reductions or "clawbacks" of social benefits like the Child Tax Benefit, which provides a monthly redistribution of income to families of modest or moderate needs.

Too technical?

Think again! Wouldn't an extra $50 or $100 a month go a long way? Doesn't it make sense to "pay yourself first?" If nothing else, learning more about simple, essential tax facts can put money in your pocket immediately . . .a rewarding pay-off for a reasonably small effort!

Unlike many other subject areas, when it comes to taxes, a little knowledge is a powerful thing. To accumulate new tax facts and put your knowledge into action is easier than you think. That's because there is a lucrative purpose behind your effort—lots more money in your pocket!

Yet there is another compelling reason to learn more about your taxes now, especially if you are an investor or pre-retiree: time is often more valuable money. How much time do you have to recover from negative economic cycles, or periods of unemployment, illness or other family concerns? One way to recover from the unexpected more quickly is to focus on your tax burden. Most Canadians give up somewhere between 22% and 45% of every dollar they make to personal income taxes. How much would you save every day if you were able to keep just 10% or 15% more? It's worth doing the calculation!

There is a time value to every dollar saved from the taxman and, as a result, every extra hour you work for yourself. Perhaps it's time to think about your "gross" earnings—the top line—and how much of it you are keeping for yourself.

It's easier than you think to focus on your favorite tax reduction strategies. We invite you now to spend a little time, to save a lot of money. Learn the basic tax reduction tips you'll need to maximize your time and money, including:

- Tips for staying onside with the tax department
- Tax tips to maximize your personal economic powerhouse: the family
- Tax reduction strategies chosen especially for employees
- Tax efficiency tips for investors and capital accumulators
- Tax advantages in family homes and vacation properties
- Significant tax saving tips for the self-employed
- Tax savings strategies for single taxpayers and seniors

You'll learn how to take home more pay, file a more accurate tax return, make better decisions about debt and investments, accumulate wealth faster, and preserve it through a lifetime of economic cycles.

Mostly you'll see that tax light: that it pays to think taxes first before making personal, career or lifestyle choices.

After all, tax reduction strategies are all about maximizing your time and your money. . .and that's what's fun about accumulating tax knowledge: it's tremendously motivating to have more of each.

This year, pull ahead. Make a commitment to pay only the correct amount of tax, and not one cent more!

ESSENTIAL TAX FACTS FOR INDIVIDUALS AND FAMILIES

Most Canadians pay too much tax all year long. Are you one of them? Do you pay more than your neighbors? Do they know something about tax savings strategies that you should know? This tax season, pledge to take back control of your after-tax dollars. It's easier than you think...you just need to know some simple tax facts:

- Arrange to pay the correct tax. . .and not one cent more
- Meet your filing obligations with CRA
- Establish and keep your residency status
- Avoid stiff penalties
- Reap a windfall with refundable tax credits
- Earn tax free income
- Earn the most tax efficient income
- Control your tax bracket and marginal tax rate
- Increase lucrative tax deductions and credits
- File for tax benefits as a family
- Recover gold on prior filed returns

Arrange to pay the correct tax. . . and not one cent more

It is your legal right and duty to arrange your affairs within the framework of the law to pay the least personal income taxes possible. For those in the know, that means more money in your pocket at tax time, and all year long.

A taxpayer's relationship with the Canada Revenue Agency (CRA) is "in your face" yet conveniently deniable at the same time. With every pay cheque, a tax remittance is made on your behalf by your employer, both to ensure you prepay your taxes for the current year, and to enable you to contribute to the Canada Pension Plan (CPP) and Employment Insurance (EI) program. So, guess who gets paid first?

Unfortunately, most people also overpay their statutory deductions-tax withholding, CPP and EI premiums with every paycheque. So you get paid second, and give the government an interest-free loan at the same time. Many self employed or passive investors, also overpay their quarterly instalment remittances. . . .

To recover your money, you have to file a tax return. . . hence the annual tax filing routine. Problem is, it's really tough to be good at something you only do once a year.

This is especially true because when it comes to tax, many people feel they are required to hit a couple of moving targets: constantly changing tax laws and interpretations—often implemented retroactively—must mesh with complicated family lives and careers which are continually in flux. Yet, mastery of your tax filing position, can catapult you and your family into a new financial stratosphere, especially when you pay yourself first, and most!

Know that our tax system is based on "self-assessment"—the onus is on you to properly assess the income, deductions and tax credits you are entitled to, and file on time, or risk expensive compliance penalties. Here's how to avoid these and become a master of self assessment.

Meet your filing obligations with CRA

The best way to save money on your taxes over the long run is to consistently file an audit-proof tax return, on time. Your legal obligation to the Canada Revenue Agency (CRA) is to pay only the correct amount of tax, no more and no less. This is legitimate tax avoidance.

The Income Tax Act is full of special "tax preferences"—preferred taxation of certain income sources to promote economic goals, tax deductions and non-refundable tax credits, which recognize different economic circumstances of the individual and family, and refundable tax credits, which redistribute income to low and middle income earners.

You can take advantage of these on a "self-assessment" basis when you file a return. What you can't do, is commit fraud or handle your tax affairs with gross negligence.

So, to begin, who must file a return? What happens if you don't? What happens if you make mistakes? How can you recover errors and omissions?

Establish and keep your residency status

The filing of a Canadian tax return rests not on citizenship, but on residency. Your Canadian residency also is what entitles you to lucrative tax deductions and refundable or non-refundable tax credits.

In today's busy world, there can be several grey areas surrounding residency for those on the go, often resulting in a case-by-case basis analysis of filing status, especially those who leave Canada temporarily. You should therefore be aware of the following definitions of residency.

Essential TAX FACT #1

Canadian residents must report "world income" in Canadian funds.

- **Individual Residency.** An individual is considered to be a resident of Canada for tax purposes if they have residential ties to Canada. These taxpayers must report world income but are eligible to claim a credit for any taxes paid to a foreign jurisdiction.

- **Deemed Residency.** Some taxpayers are considered to be residents of Canada even if they have not established residential ties. This includes individuals who:

  - Visit Canada for 183 days or more in the year
  - Work overseas as a member of the Canadian Armed Forces
  - Are a minister, high commissioner, ambassador, officer or servant of Canada

- Perform services in a foreign country under a program of the Canadian International Development Agency
- Are a member of the Canadian Armed Forces school staff
- Are a spouse or dependent child of one of the above

These taxpayers file a tax return as a normal resident.

- **Immigration and Emigration.** Those who enter the country permanently or sever all ties are considered to be "part year residents", which requires the filing of a Canadian tax return for the period of residency.

- **Non Residency.** An individual is considered to be a non-resident of Canada if residential ties to Canada have not been established, or have been severed. These individuals may still be required to file a return in Canada if they earned income from employment or self-employment here, or have disposed of certain Taxable Canadian Property—that is property that is situated in Canada, upon which the Canadian government has reserved taxation rights.

When it comes to your taxes, it's important not to leave Canada permanently in too much of a hurry. Those who sever ties permanently must first deal with a tax reconning—a departure tax will apply to most taxable assets, which must undergo valuation as at the date of departure. If such fair market valuation results in a capital gain, you'll need to square off with the tax department (cash or the posting of security will usually do).

Essential TAX FACT #2

"Departure taxes" must be calculated if you give up your Canadian residency.

Not all properties are subject to the departure tax. Specifically excluded properties include:

- pensions and similar rights including registered retirement savings plans, registered retirement income funds, and deferred profit-sharing plans

- rights to certain benefits under employee profit sharing plans, employee benefit plans, employee trusts, and salary deferral arrangements

- In the case of those who have been resident in Canada for 5 years or less, certain qualifying property that was owned at the time the person became a resident, or was inherited the taxpayer last became a resident of Canada

- employee stock options subject to Canadian tax
- interests in life insurance policies in Canada (other than segregated fund policies)

There are also special tax filing rules for the year you immigrate to Canada. For example, you will value assets as of the date of entry, so that you can avoid paying capital gains taxes on any value accrual that occurred before you became a Canadian resident. You will also qualify for refundable tax credits if you can establish residency here by December 31 of the tax year.

Immigrants or emigrants are considered to be "part year residents." In the year of entry or departure its possible to be both a Canadian resident and a "part-year non-resident" for filing purposes. Accordingly, in those years, personal amounts would be prorated for the number of days of residency, and in the case of emigrants, refundable tax credits would be denied on the final return.

It is therefore wise to receive professional advice on the tax consequences of entry or departure from Canada well in advance of your move. This can help you plan for a tax-advantaged fair market valuation date and meet all compliance requirements.

Essential TAX FACT #3

Provincial taxes are based on the province of residence on December 31.

Provincial Filing Requirements. Except for the province of Quebec, which requires the filing of a separate provincial return, all other provincial tax calculations are included in the federal tax return through additional schedules. It is important to plan moves to less expensive provinces or from more expensive provinces wisely, as your province of residency as of December 31, determines your provincial taxes for the whole year.

Avoid stiff penalties

Tax evasion is the act of making false or deceptive statements in a return, certificate, statement or answer filed or made to the CRA in order to evade

**Essential
TAX FACT #4**

Tax evasion is a crime
. . .with very expensive
consequences.

payment of tax or to willfully evade or attempt to evade compliance with the Income Tax Act. Also, to participate in destroying, altering, mutilating, or otherwise disposing of the records or books of account will be considered tax evasion.

If convicted of tax evasion, the taxpayer is liable for a fine of not less than 50% and not more than double the amount of the tax that was sought to be evaded, or imprisonment for a term not exceeding 5 years. CRA's gross negligence penalty will usually also apply for the false statement or omission of information. This amounts to 50% of tax properly payable. And of course, late filing penalties and interest could also be added if you did not file on time.

While most people dread the annual tax filing routine—it's a kind of triple negative. First, you have to spend a couple of Sundays gathering up your documentation for the whole family—that's really the hardest part.

However, this is no reason to ignore your tax filing obligations. The alternative is even more costly. That's because those who owe will face late filing penalties and interest; and lose the benefit of working with their money and investing their overpaid taxes.

**Essential
TAX FACT #5**

The tax filing deadline
is midnight April 30 for
most individuals. For the
unincorporated small
business owner it is June
15. . . but if you owe,
interest will accrue from
May 1 onward. So it
makes sense for everyone
to file by April 30.

Remember, when you fail to file, you also set yourself up for gross negligence or tax evasion penalties, on top of the interest and late filing penalties, described below:

1. First failure to file a return on time: 5% of unpaid taxes plus 1% per month up to a maximum of 12 months time from filing due date, which is June 15 for unincorporated small businesses.

2. Subsequent failure to file on time within a 3-year period: 10% of unpaid taxes plus 2% per month to a maximum of 20 months from filing due date.

Now. . .perhaps you have heard this line before from a delinquent filer: "I don't have to file on time—I'm getting a refund anyways!" This is complete folly! If you are tempted to put off filing a return for that reason, here are two questions to consider:

1. Why would you continue to give the government an interest-free loan for the use of your money, which is being eroded by inflation? (Know that you won't earn any interest on balances owed to you from CRA until 30 days after you file).

2. Why would you put yourself at risk for expensive late filing penalties if you're wrong and do owe additional taxes?

Essential TAX FACT #6

Late Filing Penalties are costly, especially for repeat offenders.

Do the simple thing and save money, too—file a tax return every year, and on time.

And there is another reason to want to file on time every year. . .to receive refundable tax credits throughout the year from the federal and provincial governments. This is especially true for low income earners or those who are not taxable, like single mothers, widows/ers or students.

Reap a windfall with Refundable Tax Credits

Many people don't know that the filing of a tax return under the Income Tax Act serves two purposes:

1. *as a means of reconciling taxes you paid throughout the year* either through employment source deductions or by instalment payments. Under our "self-assessment" system of taxation, the tax-payer is responsible for ensuring that all income, tax deductions and non-refund-able tax credits are properly claimed both on an individual and family basis.

Essential TAX FACT #7

Even those with little or no taxable income sources should file a return to receive lucrative refundable tax credits.

2. *as a way to meet social goals by redistributing income to low and middle income* earners with special family circumstances. This is done through the delivery of refundable federal tax credits like the Child Tax Benefit or Goods and Service Tax Credit, or in some provinces through provincial refundable tax credits.

Recent statistics from the Canada Revenue Agency (CRA) report over 15 million taxable filers and over 7 million non-taxable returns, filed primarily to earn *refundable tax credits*. That tells us that close to one third of Canadian tax filers understand that the tax return is an application form for lucrative credits, and that's a good thing.

Here's some more good news: you don't need to be a tax expert to benefit. Just strive to understand the *Basic Elements of the T1 General Return*. Use it as your "anchor document". All the lines you'll need to know about are addressed there, including income, deductions and tax credits you may qualify for.

Take some time to get to know its 5 Basic Elements: Identification Area, Total Income (Line 150, Net Income (Line 236), Taxable Income (Line 260) and Non-Refundable Tax Credits (See Schedule 1). These computations all lead to your refund or balance due.

Now, pick up a tax return at your local post office and have a good look for these key lines, or even better, invest in some tax software and print out the return and its schedules

Essential
TAX FACT #8

Tax software—a great investment—provides a full array of most CRA forms at the tip of your fingers.

Using tax software, you'll be able to do "what if" scenarios like an expert, and plan to save all year long. . .or at least ask better questions of your tax and financial advisors. It can really pay to learn to use software and read instructions for relevant forms carefully.

However, not all provisions appear on tax forms. For example, lucrative refundable tax credits can increase monthly cash flow—but you'll not find their calculations on the return. To receive credits like the Child Tax Benefit and the Goods and Services Tax Credit, the taxpayer and the spouse or common-law partner have to file a tax return. This is required, even if they have no income. CRA will do then calculate your eligibility for credits automatically and send any qualifying amounts directly to the applicant throughout the tax year.

But, here's what you do have to know: The value of the credits is based on combined family net income on line 236 of the tax return. And you do have some control over this number, especially with an RRSP contribution, which will be discussed in more depth in later chapters.

Now, a few more tax "secrets": You should also know that refundable credits come with accompanying "clawback zones"—income threshold levels at which refundable credits are reduced. Every dollar of family net income over those levels will reduce the benefits of the credits, which means that eligible low and middle income families falling within a clawback zone often pay a higher marginal tax rate than other wealthier families.

**Essential
TAX FACT #9**

It's good to file family tax returns together for the best tax benefits

**Essential
TAX FACT #10**

You can plan to earn exempt income sources

Finally, know that not all income sourcese are subject to tax. . .inheritances and lottery winnings are tax exempt, for example. For a complete listing of exempt income sources we invite you to visit www.knowledgebureau.com or call for a copy of Essential Tax Fact Sheets: 1-866-953-4769, toll free.

Two important exempt income sources are worth noting here.

Income from Personal Injury Award Property of a Minor. While the taxpayer was under 21 years of age, income derived from one or more of the following sources will be exempt:

- property received by or on behalf of a taxpayer as an award of damages in respect of the taxpayer's physical or mental injury,
- property substituted for such property,
- a capital gain derived from the disposition of the property or substituted property, or
- invested income that was derived from such property

Capital gains that accrue on personal injury awards up to the date of the taxpayer's 21st birthday may be exempted by electing to treat any such capital property as having been disposed of on the day immediately preceding the taxpayer's 21st birthday for its fair market value and to have been immediately re-acquired at a cost equal to those proceeds.

Income Earned on First Nations Reserves. An Indian's employment income is considered to be personal property. An Indian's employment income will usually be exempt from income tax when:

- at least 90 % of the duties of an employment are performed on a reserve,
- the employer is resident on a reserve and the Indian lives on a reserve,
- more than 50% of the duties of an employment are performed on a reserve and the employer is resident on a reserve, or the Indian lives on a reserve,
- the employer is resident on a reserve and the employer is an Indian band which has a reserve, a tribal council representing one or more Indian bands which have reserves, or an Indian organization controlled by one or more such bands or tribal councils.

When less than 90% of the duties of an employment are performed on a reserve and the employment income is not exempted by another guideline or disposition of the Act, the exemption must be prorated. The exemption will only apply to the portion of the income related to the duties performed on the reserve.

Note also that the receipt of EI benefits, retiring allowances, CPP (or QPP) payments, RPP benefits or wage loss replacement plan benefits will usually be exempt from income tax when received as a result of employment income that was exempt from tax.

Earn the most tax efficient income

Essential TAX FACT #11
All income sources are not taxed alike

Have you heard the one about the millionaire who paid no tax?

Do you have a hunch that your neighbor, who makes roughly the same gross income you do, pays less tax? Do you know why?

One of the reasons why it is difficult to compare the tax results between Canadian households with similar income levels is that income sources attract different tax rates. You and your neighbor might earn the same gross income number, but because of its source, you could be paying less in tax.

For example, you may be producing income from a consulting business, against which you can claim a series of business expenses like auto and home office costs. Your neighbor may work as an employee, with few tax write-offs to claim. You'll likely pay less tax.

Also, the tax system contains certain important provisions to meet economic, as well as social policy goals. Capital and business loss carry forward rules, for example, help those who take risks by providing a way to average income fluctuations. It's quite possible the millionaire who paid no tax this year, lost significant sums in each of the previous 10 years and was able to use those loss carry forwards to offset taxes this year, when things came together!

It is very important to diversify income sources to pay a lower overall taxes throughout your lifetime.

One of the key wealth accumulation mistakes made by those who pay too much tax their entire lifetime is that they earn income from one source only—usually employment. By diversifying your income, you can average out your tax liability, and pay less. And, when you understand how much tax the next dollar you earn attracts, it will help you arrange your efforts and your affairs towards tax efficiency.

Visit www.knowledgebureau.com to view current tax brackets and rates in Essential Tax Fact Sheets.

It should be now be apparent that the word "income" can have several different and significant meanings on the tax return, which in turn will affect your refund or balance due, and your eligibility for tax credits.

> ### Essential
> ### TAX FACT #12
>
> **Your taxes payable will be calculated on your taxable income; your refundable tax credits will be determined by the size of your net income.**

The various definitions of income on the tax return are important to note, because they will help you understand how to make income-producing decisions all year long. They can also help you with long term planning, like family income splitting. Here's an overview of the tax definitions of your income sources, so that you can plan to earn more of those which are most tax efficient:

- **Total Income (Line 150):** Includes world wide income from all sources including:

- Employment income
- Casual earnings or barter transactions
- public or private pensions
- investments that generate income from property like interest, dividends, rents or royalties
- net partnership income
- capital dispositions of assets that result in a capital gain or loss
- employment insurance benefits
- support, alimony or maintenance payments
- students in receipt of bursaries, scholarships or fellowships
- other income like payments for jury duty or Accumulated Income Payments from Registered Education Savings Plans
- Self Employment Income
- Workers compensation, social assistance, and federal supplements (ultimately deductible and not taxable, but reported to be reflected in net income, for the purposes of calculating your tax credits.)

- **Net Income (Line 236):** This number results from a series of deductions taken from Total Income on Line 150, including child care expenses, investment carrying charges and RRSP deductions. Use of these deductions to reduce net income is very significant, as Line 236 determines the level of social benefits paid under various programs including the Old Age Security, the federal refundable credits (Child Tax Benefit and the GST Credit) as well as provincial refundable credits. It is also the figure used to determine whether you can claim certain non-refundable credits for medical and charitable donations or amounts for dependants on your tax return. In the latter instance, the dependants' net income level on Line 236 is used in the determination of your claim for them.

- **Family Net Income (Line 236 of both spouses' or common law partners' returns):** This combined figure is used in the calculation of federal refundable tax credits like the Child Tax Benefit and the GST Credit and most provincial refundable credits.

- **Taxable Income (Line 260):** This number results when further deductions are taken from Net Income on Line 236, including important items like capital losses of prior years, capital gains deductions and security options deductions. The amount on Line 260 is used to calculate federal taxes, as well as provincial taxes payable.

- **Earned Income:** This refers to income from active sources like employment and self-employment, and is used to compute RRSP, disability supports and child care deduction limits. Note, however, that earned income definitions for the latter two deductions differ slightly from the definition used for RRSP contribution purposes.

There is another compelling reason to understand these terms: to avoid nasty surprises at tax time—like being unable to claim child care expenses during a period of unemployment because your family failed to meet the required "earned income" levels for those purposes—or finding out that you have actually overcontributed to your RRSP because of a low "earned income" last year. Two different definitions—two very real problems...

Such misconceptions may, in fact, come home to roost on April 30. Hopefully you won't find the need to write a big cheque, instead of receiving your expected refund, all because you didn't understand tax lingo.

Control your tax bracket and marginal tax rate

In Canada, we have a progressive tax system, which means that those who have a higher taxable income during the year generally pay higher taxes. However, the size of your tax bill can be affected by your income source as well. Tax rates are affixed to various levels of tax brackets by two different levels of government: federal and provincial, each of which require a separate tax calculation.

> **Essential TAX FACT #13**
>
> You need to know your effective and marginal tax rates.

Federal tax rates are applied uniformly to all Canadians' taxable income and are indexed for inflation each year. Provincial tax rates are applied to the same definition of taxable income, but tax brackets and rates are different and not always indexed for inflation.

See Essential Tax Fact Sheets at www.knowledgebureau.com for current tax brackets and rates.

Therefore we are interested in understanding several different types of tax rates, and in particular effective and marginal tax rates.

The effective tax rate is the average rate of tax paid on all income. Your effective tax rate takes "progressivity" into account: everyone benefits from a "tax free zone" or basic personal amount, and tax rates that will rise with your income level. You can find it easily by taking the taxes paid on Line 435 and dividing this number by your total income on line 150:

Line 435 Total Payable	$	12,820
Line 150 Total Income	$	56,393
Effective Tax Rate:	($12,820 / $56,393) = **23%**	

The marginal tax rate is the rate of tax paid on the next dollar earned. Remember, as income increases, taxes paid are proportionately greater and benefits of tax credits can be clawed back. For example:

Current income:	$	56, 393
Receipt of employment bonus:	$	1,000
Taxes payable	$	13,204
Taxes payable on prior income	$	12,820
Difference	$	375
Marginal Tax Rate:	**37.5%**	

So, you'll pay $375 more on $1000 of employment income for a total of 37.5%. This is what it costs you to earn the next like dollar.

Or, taken another way, this is how much you would save if you put that $1000 into an RRSP. It's significant—your return on the RRSP investment is a double-digit one, from a tax point of view alone. . .37.5%!

Also know that different types of income may subject to different marginal tax rates. (See Essential Tax Fact Sheets at www.knowledgebureau.com)

Increase lucrative deductions and credits

Your net income is a figure you should be come intimately familiar with. It affects so many different areas on the return. A low net income will increase refundable and non-refundable tax credits. The best way to decrease it, by the way, is to maximize your RRSP contribution.

Take a close look at the list that follows. Net Income results from the subtraction of deductions on lines 206 to 235. Do you have any of these amounts to claim?

1. Registered Pension Plan (RPP) Contributions
2. Registered Retirement Savings Plan (RRSP) Contributions
3. Annual union or professional dues
4. Child care expenses
5. Disability Supports deduction
6. Business investment losses
7. Moving expenses
8. Support payments
9. Carrying charges and interest expenses
10. Deduction for Canada Pension Plan (CPP) contributions on self employed earnings
11. Exploration and development expenses
12. Other employment expenses
13. Clergy residence deductions
14. Other deductions like certain legal fees or benefit repayments

Essential TAX FACT #14

The size of your individual net income (Line 236) will have an effect on the size of refundable and non-refundable tax credits.

Remember: A "taxable return" results when a taxable income remains after claiming allowable deductions and non-refundable tax credits. Let's define that latter term now, as you've heard it a couple of times in this chapter already and put it into perspective with your refundable tax credit opportunities.

This is of particular interest to those who support spouses, adult dependants, post-secondary students, charities or the sick and disabled. Everyone in Canada qualifies for the Basic Personal Amount—just over $8000 these days—or the first $680 or so that you earn every month.

Essential TAX FACT #15

Non-refundable tax credits are "tax preferences" provided to give recognition to the economic consequences of unique family circumstances.

In contrast to Refundable Tax Credits, which pay a cash bonus to the tax filer even if there is little or no income and no taxes paid, non-refundable tax credits reduce taxes payable only, and so do not help those who do not pay by virtue of low income. Non-refundable tax credits that you claim for your dependants are generally based on the dependant's net—not gross—income, and they may be "clawed back" if income levels rise over certain thresholds.

Review Schedule 1 of your T1 General Return for a complete listing of non-refundable tax credits available for your use. Or visit www.knowledgebureau.com to view the form.

File for tax benefits as a family

One way to file family tax returns is to prepare each return separately, calculate and send it off. That's how most people do it. This can be very costly. There are several joint, transferable or optional provisions that can be claimed on an inter-family basis. You should study these carefully:

TAX ELEMENT	PROVISION	CAN BE CLAIMED BY:
Income	–Canada Pension Plan Benefits	–After age 60, either spouse, if an assignment of split benefits has been applied for
	–Taxable Dividends	–Can be transferred to high earning spouse if Spousal Amount is created or increased.
Deductions	–Safety Deposit Box	–either spouse may claim if it holds household investment documents.
Non-Refundable Tax Credits	–Basic Personal Amount	–not transferable.
	–Age Amount, Pension Income Amount, Disability Amount, Tuition and Education Amounts	–transferrable to higher earner if lower earner is not taxable. In the case of the disability amount and tuition and education amounts this can include transfers from dependants other than spouse.
	–Claims for Spouse or Equivalent, Infirm Adults, Caregiver, Donations	–claimed by the supporting individual with higher taxable income in general.
	–Medical Expenses	–usually claimed by spouse with lower net income for best benefit.
	–Labour Sponsored Fund Tax Credit	–can be claimed by either spouse if purchased within spousal RRSP.

Keep these transferable provisions in mind when you plan tax and investment activities throughout the year and account for them at tax time. You will be in a better position to take the information from your tax return to make some important investment and lifestyle decisions:

- How can we increase the Child Tax Benefits we receive?
- Will an RRSP help?

- Should we pay down the mortgage first?
- Should we invest the Child Tax Benefits received? In whose names?
- How can we split income between family members?
- Should we borrow more money to invest in the stock market?
- Should we consider buying life insurance or fund this with our tax savings?

As you can see, the benefits of looking at your tax filing activities from a family point of view will influence your wealth accumulation activities and inter-generational estate planning. The family that files together, saves more money together.

Essential TAX FACT #16

Families make economic decisions as a unit; when you prepare taxes as a family unit, you'll get the best tax benefits.

Essential TAX FACT #17

It is important to know who is family for tax purposes.

Definition of Spouse, Common Law Partner and Dependant: Modern lifestyles have brought changes to the definition of family members connected by their tax affairs. Here's what you need to know:

A spouse, for tax purposes, is someone to whom you are legally married. A common-law partner, for tax purposes, is someone who is not your spouse but is:

- a person of the same or opposite sex with whom you lived in a relationship throughout a continuous* 12-month period, or
- someone who, at the end of the tax year, was the actual or adoptive parent of your child.

  * Separations of less than 90 days do not affect the 12-month period.

Prior to 2001, if the parties were living together for the required 12-month period at some time in the past, the Canada Revenue Agency (CRA) deemed that if they were living together again at any later time, their conjugal relationship resumed for tax purposes. This is no longer a requirement.

Dependants. Taxpayers who support both minors or adult dependants may reap tax benefits. A dependant is generally defined as:

- a child of the taxpayer,

- the taxpayer's parent or grandparent or
- under 18 years of age or wholly dependent on the taxpayer because of mental or physical infirmity.

These qualifications need not be met throughout the year but must be met at some time during the year. In claiming a dependent, the following rules must be met:

1. only one person can claim the amount for an eligible dependant in respect of the same dependant,

2. no one may claim the amount for an eligible dependant if someone else is claiming the amount for spouse or common-law partner for that dependant,

3. only one claim may be made for the amount for an eligible dependant for the same home,

4. where more than one taxpayer qualifies to make the claim, the taxpayers must agree who will make the claim or no one will be allowed to,

5. if a claim for the amount for an eligible dependant is made in respect of a dependant, no one may claim the "Amount for Infirm Dependants" or the "Caregiver Amount" in respect of the same dependant.

A taxpayer who supports a dependant who is:

- at least 18 years of age and,
- dependent on the taxpayer because of mental or physical infirmity,

may claim certain tax credits in respect of that dependant. To qualify, the dependant must be:

- the child or grandchild of the taxpayer or the taxpayer's spouse or common-law partner, or,
- the parent, grandparent, brother, sister, uncle, aunt, niece or nephew of the taxpayer or the taxpayer's spouse or common-law partner and resident in Canada at any time in the year.

**Essential
TAX FACT #18**

You can adjust prior filed returns to correct errors and omissions.

These definitions will help you co-ordinate tax filing requirements for the whole family—spouse or common law partner, minor and adult dependants.

Recovering gold on prior filed returns

It may be too good to be true...if you learn something new in reading this book and find that you have missed lucrative tax provisions on prior tax returns, you may be able to recover gold by adjusting those prior filed returns. To do so, you'll need to know about reassessment periods and CRA's Fairness Package.

And you'll want to keep your Notice of Assessment or Reassessment, which you'll receive with your refund cheque or balance due after filing your return, in a safe place, to grab important information you need to manage your tax affairs over time.

The Income Tax Act contains a definition of a "normal reassessment period", which is often referred to as the "statute of limitations" since it limits CRA's ability to reassess any tax year to the period that ends three years after the mailing of the original notice of assessment for the tax year. Under the Fairness Package, introduced in 1991, however, taxpayers could request that returns be reviewed back as far as 1985 to make adjustments for errors or omissions of most tax provisions.

To make adjustments to prior filed returns after 2004, do so within ten years after the end of the taxation year being adjusted.

This is a great way to recover "gold" from prior years. Many taxpayers miss claiming all the deductions and credits they are entitled to.

Here's how to adjust your return:

1. Review tax returns of the previous three years.

2. If you think you missed claiming something on a prior filed return, call your tax practitioner to make an adjustment or do it yourself using form T1ADJ, available on the CRA's website.

3. Have supporting documentation available in case of audit.

4. Never file a second tax return.

Remember CRA may audit tax returns to three years—the current year and two years back, unless fraud is suspected. You can avoid gross negligence or tax evasion penalties by voluntarily complying with the law to correct errors or omissions.

Also know that interest and late filing penalties may be avoided in hardship cases—like illness, death of a family member or other factor beyond the taxpayer's control. It pays to have been a "model taxpayer" when situations like this arise.

One of the best ways to leverage your "gold" from prior years' returns is to invest in an increased RRSP contribution. When you get your Notice of Reassessment with your new found money, double check the new unused RRSP contribution room that may result from the adjustment. . .then pay your financial advisor a visit.

CHAPTER SUMMATION:
ESSENTIAL TAX FILING FACTS

Filing a tax return is a historical event. Tax filing should be about reflection and perspective. In reconciling income, deductions, credits and tax payable for last year, compute your effective tax rate for the current year, contemplate what your marginal tax rate is for the future and how to make choices all year long that are tax effective. That begins with tax compliance—properly filing the return and taking advantage of all tax preferences you are entitled to. You'll want to

1. Arrange your affairs, within the framework of the law, to pay the least taxes.

2. Report "world income" in Canadian funds.

3. Anticipate "Departure taxes" if you give up your residency.

4. Plan moves around provincial tax rates by December 31.

5. Avoid the crime of tax evasion. . .which comes with very expensive consequences.

6. Avoid costly late filing penalties: File by midnight April 30

7. File even if you have little or no taxable income for lucrative tax credits

8. Invest in tax software to get forms and "what if" scenarios at your fingertips

9. File family returns together for best tax results.

10. Understand that all income sources are not taxed alike

11. Plan to earn tax exempt income sources.

12. Know your effective and marginal tax rate.

13. Beef up claims for refundable and non-refundable tax credits.

14. Understand your marginal tax rate on the next dollar earned or spent.

15. Transfer family benefits wherever possible.

16. Adjust errors or omissions on prior filed returns within ten years

NOW PUT MORE MONEY IN YOUR POCKET ALL YEAR LONG...

PERSPECTIVE

- Time is money.
- Every month in which tax is overpaid to the government is a month it doesn't work for you.
- Every month in which your after-tax dollar shrinks, your personal productivity is eroded.
- Paying tax penalties is just not smart—because it's something you can control.
- Same is true when you fail to file for available tax preferences.
- Shake yourself up—it's time to turn a new page, think about tax in a new way and take control of your after-tax results.
- By understanding the basic tax facts, you are ready for real fun: tax planning!

CHAPTER TWO

ESSENTIAL TAX FACTS FOR EMPLOYEES

A cornerstone of sound tax reduction strategies is to "pay yourself first"… especially if you are an employee. To create real wealth within your employment scenario, it also helps to tap into equity. That's why you should:

- Repeat after me. . ."A tax refund is a bad thing. . ."
- Put a tax focus on your employment negotiations
- Diversify employment income
- Negotiate the perk package
- Ensure peace of mind on health care
- Maximize tax-assisted retirement savings options
- Leverage using the employer's capital pool
- Tap into equity with employee stock option plans
- Maximize employment deductions
- Make special claims for commission salespeople
- Audit-proof auto allowances and expenses
- Write off the home office
- Tap into often-missed GST Rebates
- Claim lucrative moving expenses
- Plan for tax wise terminations

Repeat after me: "A tax refund is a bad thing. . ."

Did you know that the average tax refund in Canada is over $1200? The vast majority of Canadians overpay their taxes at tax time and all year long, to the tune of $100 a month. Why is this?

One reason is that if you are an employee, you are not the first person who gets paid for your work. Your income tax deductions come right off the top and are remitted to the government for you. You don't see it, you rarely understand how much it is, and you are likely overpaying your obligations every month. . .a fact when you get a tax refund at tax filing time.

Funny thing. . .most Canadians seem quite complacent about this. . .despite the fact that their non-deductible credit card debt is growing at the same time, and there is no extra money available to pay this or the mortgage down, or to make an RRSP contribution.

Put a tax focus on your employment negotiations

**Essential
TAX FACT #19**

Employees are restricted in the types of deductions they can claim, but tax advantages can be negotiated for bonuses, salary or wages, sabbaticals, tax free and taxable perks, retirement savings, severance packages and death benefits.

You can change all of this, by putting a tax focus on your employment negotiations. When you know the tax benefits available to you, you can file a more accurate tax return, but also, negotiate a more lucrative employment contract.

Here's the plan: let's get some extra lift out of your day-to-day efforts at your place of employment. By investing in yourself, your company, and the tax benefits available to employees under the tax system, you'll kick start your own wealth creation.

CRA defines an employer-employee relationship as follows:

> "a verbal or written agreement in which an employee agrees to work on a full-time or part-time basis for a specified or indeterminate period of time, in return for salary or wages. The employer has the right to decide where, when and how the work will be done. In this type of relationship a contract of service exists."

The employer has several obligations to meet for you in this relationship. An employer is required by law to make statutory deductions from your gross pay for contributions to the Canada Pension Plan (CPP), Employment Insurance (EI) and Income Taxes.

These must be remitted usually once a month, although very small businesses have the option to remit each quarter. Minors need not contribute to the Canada Pension Plan; nor do those over 70 (except in Quebec) or in receipt of CPP benefits. Everyone who is employed and earns more than $2000 in the year, must contribute to EI, that is, there is no age limit.

It is also a requirement that the employer prepare a T4 slip for each employee and issues it to the employee by the end of February each year, for use in filing the income tax return. One copy is remitted to CRA at this time as well.

But that T4 Slip can contain so much more information:

- Commission income against which employment expenses can be claimed
- Deductible union or professional dues
- Deductible contributions to company pension plans
- Deductible charitable donations
- Deductible medical premiums to private health care plans
- Perks that can be offset with tax deductions like Northern Residents Deductions, auto expenses, carrying charges for low-interest investment loan benefits, Securities Options Deductions, Home Relocation Loan Deductions, RRSP contributions and rollovers; deductions for Worker's Compensation Benefits received

Essential TAX FACT #20

Proper completion of the Personal Tax Credit Return and its sister, Form T1213 Request to Reduce Tax Deductions at Source will help you pay the right amount of tax all year long.

And, it is up to the employee to claim the correct tax credits and deductions to increase the amount of tax withholding that is returned at the end of the year when the tax return is filed. In fact, you can apply to get the benefit of those increased tax refunds immediately.

You may be familiar with the *TD1 Tax Credit Return*. It's a form you'll complete every time you start a new job, to let your employer know how much to withhold from your pay for income taxes. It is based on non-refundable tax credits, like your basic personal amount, spousal amounts, caregiver amounts, tuition and education amounts and the deduction for Northern Residents, and allows you to direct increased tax deductions to cover other income sources you may have during the year.

It will not, however, take into account other tax deductible expenditures you may have all year long like RRSP contributions, deductible alimony, significant interest costs, rental losses, child care, commission sales or other expenses of employment, medical expenses or large charitable donations. For these purposes, you need to file *Form T1213*.

This form will allow you to ask that less tax be taken from your earnings—a wise move if you want to pay off non-deductible credit card debt or your mortgage, or kick start a more aggressive savings plan. This is the first and best way for you to put more money in your pocket all year long.

Grab these forms off the internet, from your human resource department, or ask your tax or financial advisors to help you.

**Essential
TAX FACT #21**

Another reason employees overpay their taxes is because they don't diversify their income sources.

Diversify employment income

Now that you have taken control of your after-tax employment dollars, it's important to reframe your thinking around your master-servant relationship. You can earn equity as well as employment income, with proper tax planning. There are just a few basics you'll need to know.

There are several sources of employment income within a master-servant relationship:

- Income from salary or wages, which is taxable in the year received
- Director's fees (these are subject to CPP but not EI premiums)
- Employee Benefit Plans like self-funded leave of absence
- The value of taxable benefits or perks

Employment income is always reported on the cash basis—when received. The employee will also report on a calendar year basis—January to December—in every case. Sometimes, an opportunity for salary deferral to a following year may be available.

Under a salary deferral arrangement, receipt of salary or wages is postponed into the future; generally the next tax year. However, here's a trap: the deferred amount is generally included in income in the current year or year of contribution—which means that no tax deferral is actually allowed.

More common and allowable salary deferral can be achieved through a registered plan:

- Registered Pension Plan (RPP)
- Employee Profit Sharing Plan (EPSP)
- Deferred Profit Sharing Plan (DPSP)

In addition, it is possible to defer salary or wages under a self-funded leave or sabbatical. The employee who saves in this way will not be subject to tax in the year the leave is earned as long as salary is deferred for no more than 6 years and no more than 1/3 of the salary is deferred. The leave of absence must start in the 7th year and must be for a period of at least six months. The employee must then return to work for at least the same amount of time as the leave. The amounts are taxable in the year withdrawn.

You should also be aware that there are numerous types of employee benefit plans available. Often the employee will not be taxed when contributions are made to these types of plans, but benefits received from them are generally taxable when received. This can include income from registered pension plans, group sickness or accident plans, supplementary employment plans, deferred profit sharing plans, wage loss replacement plans, and certain employee trusts.

Therefore, while employment income is usually taxable as received, a few special tax preferences exist to help the employee defer some compensation into the future. Tap into this wherever you can. But start with a good, long term contract and a substantial perk package.

Negotiate the perk package

Taxable benefits are already included in income in Box 14 of the T4 slip so there is no need to add them to income again when you prepare a return. This is a common tax filing error. Taxable benefits include:

- Board and lodging at fair market value
- Rent-free and low-rent housing
- Travel benefits for the employee and his/her family
- Personal use of an employer-provided vehicle
- The value of holidays, prizes, and other awards
- Frequent flyer program points used for personal use if earned on business trips
- Premiums under provincial hospital plans
- Interest-free or low-interest loans
- The cost of relocation benefits, for example, reimbursement for losses suffered on sale of an old residence, but only one half the amounts over $15,000 must be added to income.

You should also know that certain taxable benefits qualify for deductions on the tax return. These include:

- **Housing, Board and Lodging:** which can include cleric's housing allowance, rent-free or low-rent apartments provided to caretakers or subsidized meals or travel in a prescribed zone or for medical travel. Board and lodging provided at a remote or special worksite can be received tax free, however. Offsetting deductions may be included for clerics or those who qualify for the northern residents' deduction.

- **Personal use of employer's auto:** An automobile "standby charge" is calculated to provide a taxable benefit to recognize the personal use component of an employer-provided vehicle. It is calculated at 2 per cent per month of the original cost of the vehicle where the employer owns the vehicle, or two-thirds of the lease payment for leased vehicles. However for car sales persons, the benefit is $1^1/2$%.

- **Operating Costs.** Amounts paid for the operation of the employer's vehicle will also be taxable as a benefit, unless they are reimbursed by the employee within 45 days after the end of the tax year. The benefit is determined as a flat per kilometre rate, regardless of how or how much the employer paid for the expenses. This rate is announced every year in December. Alternatively, the benefit can be assessed at one half the normal stand-by charge.

- **Reduction in Standby Charges.** It is possible that the employee may offset this benefit with a claim for Employment Expenses using Form T777 Employment Expenses or through a reduction in standby charges if personal driving is less than 20,000 kilometers per year and the car is used more than 50% of the time for employment related use.

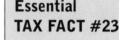

Essential TAX FACT #23

Employees should discuss the reduction of standby charges with their payroll department.

- **Interest-Free Loans and Low Interest Loans:** A deduction for carrying charges may be possible if an employer-provided loan is used by the employee for investment purposes. This might result, for example, if the employee borrowed to invest in company shares.

- **Employee home relocation loan deduction:** a deduction may be possible on Line 248. This is discussed in more detail later.

- **Securities Options Deductions:** a deduction may be possible on Line 249 for those who have generated a taxable benefit from employee stock option purchases and disposals. See details below.

- **Other taxable benefits,** including amounts included in income for health or educational benefits received may qualify for non-refundable credits on the personal tax return – such as medical expenses or tuition and education amounts.

Essential TAX FACT #24

Employment Commissions included in income may be offset by Employment Expenses on Line 229 and the GST Rebate on Line 457 under certain conditions.

- **Cost of Tools.** Where an employer makes payments to its employees to offset the cost of tools required to perform their work, the amount of the payment must be included in the employees' incomes. However, an offsetting deduction is allowed for the cost of an apprentice mechanic's tools.

Many employees also fail to negotiate for lucrative tax free benefits from their employer. *For a complete list of tax benefits visit www.knowledgebureau.com.*

Essential TAX FACT #25

Employer-paid education costs could be received tax free.

Essential TAX FACT #26

Other benefits may be taxable, but subject to exceptions that provide for tax free results.

Essential TAX FACT #27

Frequent Flyer Points used personally by employees will usually be taxable.

• **Employer-Paid Educational Costs.** When training is paid for by the employer for courses taken primarily for the benefit of the employer, there is no taxable benefit. However, a taxable benefit arises when the training is primarily for the benefit of the employee. Amounts included in the taxpayer's income for tuition will be eligible for the tuition tax credit if they would have been eligible had they been paid by the employee.

• **Financial Counselling and Income Tax Return Preparation.** Financial counselling services or income tax return preparation provided directly or indirectly by an employer normally produce a taxable benefit to the employee who receives the benefit. However, financial counselling services in respect of the re-employment or the retirement of an employee will not result in a taxable benefit to the employee.

• **Frequent Flyer Points.** CRA takes the position that where an employee accumulates frequent flyer points while travelling on employer-paid business trips and uses them to obtain air travel or other benefits for the personal use of the employee or the employee's family, the fair market value of such air travel or other benefits must be included in the employee's income. Where an employer does not control the credits accumulated in a frequent flyer program by an employee while travelling on employer-paid business trips, it will be the responsibility of the employee to determine and include in income the fair market value of any benefits received or enjoyed. This value can be computed as the lowest equivalent ticket price on the flight.

Essential TAX FACT #28

An employee can receive up to $500 in non-cash gifts from the employer, tax free.

- **Gifts Under $500.** A gift (either in cash or in kind) from an employer to an employee is a benefit derived during or because of the individual's employment. However, since October 24, 2001, an employer is allowed to give to an employee two tax-free, non-cash gifts commemorating a wedding, Christmas or similar occasion or in recognition of service or the reaching of a milestone and still claim those costs as an expense in computing taxable income.

Essential TAX FACT #29

Gifts containing corporate logos may have insignificant tax consequences.

When an employee is rewarded by an employer with merchandise or other non-cash items, the fair market value of the award must be included in the employee's income. If an item is personalized with a corporate logo or engraved with the employee's name or a message, the fair market value of the item may be negatively affected. In such cases, the amount to be included in the employee's income may be reduced by a reasonable amount, having regard to all the circumstances. Depending on the value of a particular award, the existence of a logo may have little, if any, impact on the fair market value of the item. When the award given is a plaque, trophy or other memento of nominal value for which there is no market, it is not necessary to include any amount in an employee's income as a taxable benefit.

- **Vacations.** Where an employer pays for a vacation for an employee, and/or the employee's family, the cost is considered to be a taxable benefit to the employee.

In such cases, there is a taxable benefit equivalent to the fair market value of the accommodation less any amount which the employee paid

Essential TAX FACT #30

After June 1994, premiums paid for group term life insurance are considered to be a full taxable benefit.

Essential TAX FACT #31

Taxable vacations include the use of the employer's vacation property by an employee, the employee's family or both.

for the use of the property to the employer. The taxable benefit may be reduced if there is conclusive evidence to show that the employee was involved in business activities for the employer during the vacation.

In a situation where an employee's presence is required for business purposes and this function is the main purpose of the trip, no benefit will be associated with the employee's travelling expenses necessary to accomplish the business objectives of the trip if the expenditures are reasonable in relation to the business function.

Where a business trip is extended to provide for a paid holiday or vacation, the employee is in receipt of a taxable benefit equal to the costs borne by the employer with respect to that extension.

Note that where a spouse accompanies an employee on a business trip the payment or reimbursement by the employer of the spouse's travelling expenses is a taxable benefit to the employee unless the spouse was, in fact, engaged primarily in business activities on behalf of the employer during the trip.

- **Relocation Costs.** If an employer reimburses an employee for a loss suffered by the latter in selling the family home upon being required by the employer to move to another locality or upon retirement from employment in a remote area, only a portion of the reimbursement must be included in income as a taxable benefit.

Essential TAX FACT #32

Reimbursement of up to $15,000 of losses on the sale of an employee's home may be tax free, where the employer required the move.

Where the loss and reimbursement are both less than $15,000 no taxable benefit will accrue. Where the loss and re-imbursement exceed $15,000 the benefit is one-half of the excess of the lesser of the loss and the reimbursement over $15,000.

- **Employer-Paid Parking.** Parking costs paid by the employer will generally be included as a taxable benefit of an office or employment, calculated at fair market value, however they are excluded in the value of a stand-by charge, or auto operating expense benefits, or benefits for disabled employees. However, recent court challenges have found favour with the taxpayer in establishing a non-taxable status for parking, when it was found to be in the employer's favour to offer parking to employees.

Ensure peace of mind on health care

The tax status of premiums paid and benefits received from employer-sponsored group and non-group health plans can be confusing, but is very important in the overall scheme of compensation to the employee. These plans can provide important peace of mind when expensive health care costs arise.

Taxable Status of Premiums Paid. Premiums will be taxable in two instances: where the employer pays or reimburses the employee for the employee portion of premiums to a provincial health care plan, or where an employer pays the premium under a non-group plan that is a wage loss replacement, sickness or accident insurance plan, a disability insurance plan, or an income maintenance insurance plan, the payment of the premium is regarded as a taxable benefit to the employee. This is true whether the employer paid some or all of the premiums. Payroll source deductions made for the payment of the premiums are considered to be payments made by the employee not the employer.

If the wage loss replacement plan is a group plan, or if the health care plan is private, then the employer's portion of the premiums paid is not considered to be a taxable benefit.

Taxable Status of Benefits Received. If the employee paid all of the premiums to a wage loss replacement plan, then periodic payments received (or a lump sum paid in lieu of periodic payments) from the plan are tax-free and should not be reported on an information slip.

If the plan was funded, in whole or in part, by the employer, then the benefits received are taxable, but the employee is entitled to a deduction for all premiums that he has paid since 1968 and not previously deducted. The deduction should be claimed on Line 229 of the tax return.

Maximize tax-assisted retirement savings options

An employer may assist the employee in maximizing retirement savings using the tax department as an active participant in wealth accumulation. There are numerous ways to do so.

Begin, by adjusting source deductions for income taxes on each payroll period to take into account the deductible portion of employee contributions to Registered Pension Plans (RPPs), and Registered Retirement Savings Plans (RRSPs), as discussed in Chapter 1. Then know the details of tax deferred accumulation, severance rollovers and withdrawal. Here are some basic rules:

Registered Pension Plans. A registered pension plan (RPP) is a private pension plan set up for employees, which has been registered by the Minister of National Revenue. The plan may be instituted by the employer or a trade union association in cooperation with the employer. The employer must make contributions to the plan. The plan may be structured as a defined benefit or a money purchase arrangement or a combination of the two. It is important as you negotiate a new employment contract, to find out the details.

Under a *money purchase* plan the employer and employee contributions in each member's separate account accumulates investment earnings on a tax-deferred basis and the sum total at the end determines the size of pension benefits that can be purchased for the employee at retirement. There is no promise that a certain level of retirement benefits will be provided and no uncertainty regarding the employer's financial obligation to the plan.

A *defined benefit plan* on the other hand, is a plan under which the ultimate retirement benefits promised are determined by formula. The employee's contributions are therefore predetermined; and the employer would generally contribute whatever is required to ensure those promised retirement benefits materialize.

An employee may make contributions to an RPP:

- for the current year or
- for past service for years after 1990

Current Year Employee Contributions. These amounts are tax deductible and appear in Box 20 of the T4 slip or on a union dues receipt. They are only deductible in the current tax year and may not be carried over to another taxation year.

Past Service Contributions for Service Before 1990. In addition, taxpayers may deduct, within limits, their contributions to an RPP in respect of service in years before 1990. Such amounts are included in Box 20, 74 and 75 of the employee's T4 slip. The deduction limitations are complicated, as shown below:

- *Employee contributions for pre-l990 past service while not a contributor* – An employee may deduct the least of:
  - contributions made in the year or a previous year in respect of such service less deductions previously claimed
  - $3,500
  - $3,500 per year of such service to which the employee has made past service contributions minus deductions previously claimed in respect of those contributions and deductions claimed before 1987 for "additional voluntary contributions"

- *Employee contributions for pre-1990 past service while a contributor* – Deduct the lesser of:
  - The amount of the contributions made in the year, or a previous year, less deductions previously claimed

- $3,500 minus the amount deducted in the year for
  - current service
  - post-1989 past service contributions and
  - pre-1990 past service contributions while not a contributor

Essential TAX FACT #36

Any such past service contributions that are not deductible may be carried forward to a subsequent year and deducted with the same limitations.

Again, any amounts contributed but not deductible may be carried forward to a subsequent year and deducted with the same limitations.

A taxpayer's eligibility to claim undeducted past service contributions carried forward is not affected by changes in employment status. That is, the taxpayer may retire or change companies and still be allowed to deduct past service pension plan contributions carried forward.

Pension Adjustments. This is a term you need to know. Employees who are members of a Registered Pension Plan will be assigned a Pension Adjustment for the year. This is reported in Box 52 of the T4 slip or Box 34 of the T4A slip. You should also know that employees who contribute in respect of past service will be assigned a "Past Service Pension Adjustment" (PSPA).

Note that benefits received from a registered pension plan are taxable. In some cases, they may qualify for the Pension Income Amount.

See next chapter for more details on the Registered Retirement Savings Plan (RRSP) and its contribution limits—an important cornerstone of retirement savings employees will want to tap into to supplement their superannuation in retirement.

Leverage using the employer's capital pool

Employees should always strive to build capital—assets that can produce other sources of income or grow in value. One way to do so is to use your employer's money—at preferred low or no-interest rates. This however, will give rise to a taxable benefit.

For example, the employer may loan funds to the employee or the employee's spouse. In either case, a taxable benefit would accrue to the taxpayer, unless the spouse is also an employee of the same employer. The same rules will apply when the employee receives a loan from a third party, if the employer is involved in securing the loan for the employee.

The amount of the benefit is equal to:

- the interest on the loan at CRA's currently prescribed rate
- any payments made by the employer less
- amounts of interest paid back to the employee to the employer either during the year or within 30 days after the end of the year.

This benefit is included in the taxpayer's income and will be reported on the T4 issued by the employer.

The taxable benefit will not apply where the interest rate on the loan is equal to or greater than a commercial rate so long as the interest is actually paid by the debtor. Special rules apply to housing loans and home relocation loans, discussed later.

Note: These rules apply to shareholders as well as to employees. The difference between a shareholder loan and an employee loan is that the benefit accrues to the employee, even if the loan is to someone else. However, the benefit accrues to the debtor if the loan is a shareholder loan.

This is because of a special anti-avoidance rule that prevents a shareholder from indefinitely postponing the recognition of dividend income from a corporation by taking continuous shareholder loans. Professional help should be sought to properly report these transactions.

Essential TAX FACT #40

If the employer-provided loan was used to acquire income-producing investments, the amount of the interest benefit shown on the T4 will be deductible as a carrying charge.

Essential TAX FACT #41

It is important to determine if the loan was granted because the taxpayer was an employee or a shareholder of the company

Essential TAX FACT #42

Where the employer-provided loan is forgiven or settled for an amount less than the amount outstanding, forgiven amount must be included in the taxpayer's income.

Where the shareholder is also an employee, certain loans will be allowed the same treatment given to any employee if it can be established that bona fide loan arrangements are made, the loan is repaid over a reasonable period of time and the loan is a direct result of the employer-employee relationship. This means that the company must make such loans available to all employees.

Tap into equity with employee stock option plans

Employees may be presented with an opportunity to purchase shares in the employer's corporation at some future date, but at the market price of the shares at the time the option was granted. This is known as the exercise price.

Essential TAX FACT #43

There are no tax consequences when the option is granted.

However, when the employee exercises these stock or security options a taxable benefit arises, equal to the difference between the market value of the shares purchased and the previous exercise price.

When is this taxable? It depends on the type of corporation.

If the employer is a Canadian Controlled Private Corporation (CCPC), the taxable benefit is deemed to arise when the employee disposes of the shares.

In the case of a public corporation, the taxable benefit arises when the employee exercises the option.

Note this important date: You must express your intention to defer the security options benefits to your employer by January 16 of the year after the year in which the option is exercised, so that the deferred amount may be included on your T4 slip.

The taxable benefit may not be deferred if you:

- emigrate from Canada or
- in the year of death.

It is wise to get some professional help before stock options are acquired or disposed of, as certain technical provisions, including orders of disposition must be observed. Also, when an employee disposes of shares acquired as the result of exercising a stock option and then disposes of the shares within 30 days of acquiring them, it is possible to elect that the special disposition ordering rules do not apply. Special rules also apply to the donation of such employer-provided stock options.

**Essential
TAX FACT #44**

For options exercised after February 27, 2000, employees may defer up to $100,000 of benefits until the shares are disposed of by filing *Form T1212* with the tax return each year.

Maximize employment deductions

**Essential
TAX FACT #45**

When the taxable benefit is included in income, the employee is also eligible for the Securities Options Deduction which is equal to one-half of the taxable benefit.

The *Income Tax Act* is very specific about the expenses that may be claimed by employees. Employment deductions are generally claimed on *Form T777 Employment Expenses* and require the completion and signing of *Form T2200 Declaration of Conditions of Employment* by the employer.

Special, more generous deductions are allowed for the commission sales employee. Those who earn salary only may deduct the following out-of-pocket expenses, but only up to the amount of their earnings from employment; no carry over of deductions is allowed to the following year with the exception of home workspace expenses. See Fact

Visit www.knowledgebureau.com for Essential Tax Fact Sheets on the details of employment expenses and special rules for artists and musicians.

**Essential
TAX FACT #46**

Long distance truckers and other employees in the transport business may deduct certain unreimbursed board and lodging expenses.

If an employee of an airline, rail company, trucking company or other such organization must:

- regularly travel away from the municipality or metropolitan area where their home terminal is located, and

- use vehicles provided by their employers to transport goods or passengers.

It is possible to claim the cost of meals using one of two methods:

- the "simplified method": here unreceipted claims can be made for one meal every four hours from check-out time, up to a maximum of three meals per 24-hour period at a flat rate per meal. Currently, this is $15.00 per meal (Maximum $45.00 per 24 hour period). For trips in the US, the amount is $15 US. The rate from 1990 to 2002 was $11 Can. per meal.

- the "detailed method," whereby claims are made according to actual receipts submitted.

Essential TAX FACT #47

Only one-half of the amount of meal costs is deductible, but the full cost of lodging while away from home is also deductible (with receipts).

Note: Workers on scheduled runs of ten hours or less are expected to eat before and after work and therefore may only claim one meal per day. Special rules also apply for crews of workers who are provided cooking facilities. Under the "batching method", receipts are not required but the claim is limited to $30.00 per day (starting in 2003).

Employees who claim deductible expenses, including the *Claim for Board and Lodging* (which requires completion of *Form TL2* and signature by the employer) may receive a rebate of the GST/HST paid, discussed later. These amounts are added to income in the year received. The employee must support the claims with time and distance logs.

Make special claims for commission salespeople

Employees who earn their living negotiating contracts for their employers or selling on commission may claim expenses for travel and sales costs under these circumstances:

- they are required to pay their own expenses
- they regularly perform their duties away from their employer's place of business
- they do not receive a tax-free travel allowance.

Deductible Travel Expenses allowed include:

- automobile-related operating expenses like gas, oil, repairs and fixed costs like licenses, insurance, interest, leasing and Capital Cost Allowance. The latter three expenses are limited to certain annual maximums if a passenger or luxury vehicle is used. This is discussed in more detail later.

- the cost of air, bus, rail, taxi or other transportation which takes the employee outside the employer's metropolitan area.

Deductible Sales Expenses allowed include promotional expenses, entertainment expenses (subject to the 50% restriction), travel, auto and home office costs.

Note: Employees are not allowed to make a claim for capital expenditures with the exception of the purchase of vehicles, musical instruments or aircraft. Therefore it is more tax efficient to lease computers, cell phones or other equipment, or ask the employer to pay for these.

Essential TAX FACT #48

When travel expenses only are claimed, the amounts may exceed commissions earned and excess expenses may offset other income of the year.

Essential TAX FACT #49

Sales Expenses may exceed commissions earned in the calendar year except for interest and capital cost allowance on a motor vehicle.

Audit-proof auto allowances and expenses

Auto Allowances. When an employee receives an additional amount as an auto allowance from an employer, in addition to salary or wages, the amounts will generally be taxable, unless the amount is "reasonable". Reasonable Tax Free Travel Allowances include:

- Travel allowances paid to members of the Canadian Forces,

- Reasonable allowances for travel expenses paid to a commission salesman,

- Reasonable allowances for travel expenses paid to a clergyman,

- Reasonable allowances for use of a motor vehicle paid to an employee for travel in the performance of the employee's duties.

- Reasonable allowances received by Members of Parliament

In addition, the employee must not be reimbursed for actual expenditures (Exception: the employer may reimburse for supplementary insurance charges, toll or ferry charges). Amounts paid to part-time employees (such as visiting professors) may also qualify under these rules, as long as the employer and employee:

- are dealing at arm's length
- the employee had other employment or was self-employed and
- the duties of employment were performed more than 80 kilometres from the employee's residence and other employment/self-employment.

Reasonable amounts paid in advance (on a periodic basis) by the employer may also be excluded from income if:

- they are based on distance travelled (i.e. a cents per kilometre basis),
- the rate is reasonable,
- the employee is required to report distance travelled for business purposes and,
- there is a year-end reconciliation of distance travelled to amounts advanced and the employee is required to repay any excess amounts received.

A prescribed per kilometre rate is generally stated by CRA each year as the reasonable rate to use in calculating these amounts.

Where the allowance is not a reasonable amount the whole amount of the allowance is included in computing the employee's income and, if the employee qualifies, an appropriate amount may be deducted for travel expenses.

Special rules also exist for those employed at a remote worksite.

Auto Expenses. Auto expenses are one of the most common deductions for the employed and self-employed yet, also amongst the most audited. Therefore it is important to understand the rules surrounding "mixed use".

Personal use includes vehicle use by other family members, friends, etc. and travel to and from the place of business or employment.

To make the claim on a tax return, total expenses are first totalled, as per the actual receipts and or log of cash expenditures like car washes or parking meters. Then the total amount expended and so supported, is pro-rated by the portion of business/employment kilometres over the total kilometres driven in the year.

Automotive expenses can only be deducted if they are not reimbursed by the employer or business. If they are reimbursed, but the amount of the reimbursement is not reasonable, the reimbursement can be shown as income and the actual auto expenses otherwise deductible (as discussed above) can be deducted in computing net income.

Eligible employees must pay their own auto expenses and be required to use their vehicle in carrying out duties of employment. *Form T2200* must be signed by the employer.

**Essential
TAX FACT #52**

For those who use their vehicle for both personal and business/employment purposes, it is necessary to keep an auto log that records distance driven for both purposes.

**Essential
TAX FACT #53**

Only parking costs can be claimed in full. No "cents-per-kilometer" claims are allowed.

**Essential
TAX FACT #54**

There are two types of auto expenses that can be claimed: fixed or operating costs.

Operating costs include gas, oil, maintenance, repairs, insurance and auto club memberships . However other "fixed" expenses are subject to restrictions; specifically these are Capital Cost Allowance or CCA, leasing or interest costs. This happens when the taxpayer acquires a passenger or luxury vehicle—that is, a vehicle with a capital cost of more than $30,000 plus taxes or for which a lease of more than $800 plus taxes is paid per month. Also restricted are interest costs—a maximum of $300 a month or $10 per day is allowed under current rules.

For the purposes of claiming Capital Cost Allowance, these vehicles are scheduled in Class 10.1, which essentially carries only one asset per Class. Other vehicles (including those known as motor vehicles and autos which are not passenger vehicles) are placed in Class 10, which features a "pooling" of capital costs.

In each Class 10 and Class 10.1, the undepreciated capital cost qualifies for a 30% CCA rate, and all other deductibility rules are similar, including a special half-year rule on acquisition. However, aside from the restriction on the capital cost itself, there are several differences in tax results when the asset is disposed of. What you need to know, before you buy or lease a vehicle is this that passenger or luxury vehicles will result in a restricted claim for CCA, interest or leasing costs and this tax result should be taken into account before you buy or lease.

See Chapter 5 for a more detailed discussion of how to make capital cost allowance claims. Visit www.knowledgebureau.com for more information on keeping auto logs.

Write off the home office

Many employees and self-employed work out of their home and may make legitimate claims for the cost of running a home workspace. What is again important is to prorate total costs to remove any personal use component by the following fraction:

$$\frac{\text{Square footage of the home workspace}}{\text{Square footage of the entire living area}} \quad x \quad \begin{array}{c} \text{Total} \\ \text{Eligible} \\ \text{Expenses} \end{array} \quad = \quad \begin{array}{c} \text{Deductible} \\ \text{Expense} \end{array}$$

Essential TAX FACT #55

Non-deductible home office expenses may be carried forward (indefinitely) to reduce income from that employer in subsequent years.

Claims by Employees. An employee may not claim home office expenses in excess of income from employment.

In order to claim home office expenses an employee must have a *Form T2200* signed by the employer to certify that the employee is required to maintain the home office and pay the expenses of operating it. Employees' claims for home office expenses are made on *Form T777 Statement of Employment Expenses.*

Claims by the Self-Employed. In the case of the self-employed, the space must be:

- used exclusively to earn business income on a regular and continuous basis for the purposes of meeting clients of the business, or
- the principal place of business.

Restriction on Home Workspace Expenses. The self-employed may claim these expenses, provided that they do not increase or create an operating loss. If they do, reduce net income from the business to zero with these expenses and then claim balance next year. This carry forward is indefinite and may be used against future income from the business enterprise, so track it carefully. Make the claim for self-employed taxpayers on the home workspace section of the business statement (T2032, T2042, T2121, or T2124).

See www.knowledgebureau.com for a list of Deductible Home Workspace Expenses.

Tap into often-missed GST Rebates

Employees who claim employment expenses on Line 229 or union and professional dues on Line 212 and who are not in receipt of a reasonable auto allowance for those expenses may apply for a cash rebate of any GST or HST paid on these expenses on Line 457 of the tax return. Form GST-370 must be completed.

Expenses eligible for the rebate include:

- office expenses
- travel expenses
- entertainment expenses
- meals and lodging
- motor vehicle expenses
- leasing costs
- parking cost

- miscellaneous supplies (e.g. street maps, stamps, pens, pencils, and paper clips), and
- capital cost allowance on motor vehicles, aircraft, and musical instruments acquired after 1990.

In the case of GST, the rebate is 7/107 of the expenses on which GST was paid. In the case of HST, the rebate is 15/115 of the expenses.

Essential TAX FACT #58

Taxpayers who have failed to claim the *GST/HST Rebate on Form GST-370* in prior years may file adjustments to recover this credit for the prior 10 year period.

When the GST/HST rebate is received, the portion that relates to current expenses must be reported as income on Line 104 in the year received. The portion that relates to a capital asset (vehicle, musical instrument or airplane) must be used to reduce the UCC of the class to which the asset belongs.

Claim lucrative moving expenses

Lucrative moving deductions can be claimed on Line 219 and Form T1M. To qualify, the taxpayer must earn salary, wages, or self-employment income at the new location. In addition, the taxpayer must stop working or operating a business at the old location, and establish a new home where the taxpayer and family will reside.

Essential TAX FACT #59

To be eligible, the new home must be at least 40 km closer to the new work location than the old home.

The following income sources earned at the new location will not be considered "qualifying income" for the purposes of claiming moving expenses:

- investment income
- employment insurance benefits
- other income sources, except student awards (see below).

The distance is measured by the shortest normal route open to the travelling public. Generally the move must be within Canada although students may claim moving expenses to attend a school outside Canada if they are otherwise eligible. See Chapter 4.

Expenses for moves between two locations outside Canada may be possible if the taxpayer is a deemed resident or factual resident of Canada and the move was taking place from the place the taxpayer ordinarily resided, to a new place where the taxpayer will ordinarily reside.

Visit www.knowledgebureau.com for a list of deductible and non-deductible moving expenses.

This method does not require receipts to be kept for travel expenses, only a record of the distance traveled during the move. The rate is calculated based on the province in which the move began. Meals en route may also be charged at a flat rate per meal ($11.00 at the time of writing) with a maximum of three meals per day (total $33.00). For ongoing current rates, visit the CRA web site at http://www.ccra-adrc.gc.ca/travelcosts.

Note: Taxpayers who receive reimbursements for moving expenses may only deduct expenses if the amount received as a reimbursement is included in income, or if the amounts claimed are reduced by the amount of the reimbursement.

Employee Home Relocation Deduction. When an employer relocates an employee to another area, the employer may offer the employee a low-interest or no-interest loan to assist with the costs of relocating. The difference between the interest charged on the loan and the interest calculated at the prescribed interest rate is a taxable benefit and included on the employee's T4 Slip. Recipients of this benefit may qualify for the Employee Home Relocation Loan Deduction claimed on Line 248.

If the term of repayment for the home relocation loan is more than five years, the balance owing at the end of five years (from the day the loan was made) is considered a new loan. The taxable benefit will be calculated as if

Essential TAX FACT #60

Travel expenses may be calculated using a rate per kilometre basis rather than claiming the actual amount spent. Meals can be claimed on a flat rate, too.

Essential TAX FACT #61

If income at the new location does not sufficiently offset all moving expenses in the year of the move, expenses may be carried forward and applied against income at the new location in the following year or years.

Essential TAX FACT #62

The home relocation loan deduction is available for the first five years of the loan, and is equal to the taxable benefit charged the employee the loan was made at that time. However, in this case, no home relocation loan deduction is available.

The rules for the calculation of benefits for a home relocation loan are similar as for any employer-provided loan. The difference, is that for a home purchase loan and a home relocation loan, the prescribed interest rate used for the calculation of the taxable benefit is the rate in effect at the time the loan is made.

Plan for tax wise terminations

All good things may one day come to and end. When it comes to the end of the road with your employer, consider these tax consequences of termination:

1. **Plan a tax free rollover of your termination or severance into an RRSP:** The amount eligible for rollover to your (but not your spouse's) RRSP, depends upon when service was provided to the employer:
   - For service after 1995, *no amount* of severance can be rolled over to an RRSP and therefore the full amount is exposed to income taxes.
   - For service *after 1988 and before 1996*, a single limit of $2,000 per year of service can be rolled over.
   - For service *before 1989*, it is possible to roll over $2,000 for each year of service plus $1,500 for each year in which none of the employer's contributions to a company pension plan vested in the employee.

Remember, if you can't rollover any amounts by virtue of employment after 1996, top up unused RRSP contribution room and take this deduction against the exposed income. Then, plan to make any taxable withdrawals from the RRSP as required while you hunt for new work; hopefully this will happen, for tax purposes, in a year in which income falls into a lower tax bracket.

Also, the possibility of taking severance over two taxation years should be explored to determine whether the tax brackets and rates at which the income will be taxed can be reduced, and whether eligibility for social benefits, like the Child Tax Benefit, can be created.

2. **EI Maximization.** Employment Insurance benefits you may receive throughout the year post-employment, may be clawed back when you file your income tax return, if your net income for the tax year is

$48,750 or higher. This can be avoided with astutely planned RRSP contributions.

3. **CTB Creation.** Many high income earners who find themselves unemployed often fail to plan for new eligibility for Child Tax Benefits, because they perhaps didn't qualify for them in the past. These refundable monthly payments are maximized at family net income levels just over $35,000, but can be paid partially if income is above this, depending on the number of children in the home.

4. **Medical Expense Deductibility.** Taxpayers often forget that group health benefits end with employment. Negotiate for continuation wherever possible.

CHAPTER SUMMATION:
ESSENTIAL TAX FACTS FOR EMPLOYEES

1. Employees are restricted in the types of deductions they can claim, but tax advantages can be negotiated for:
   - bonuses, salary or wages,
   - sabbaticals,
   - tax free and taxable perks,
   - retirement savings,
   - severage packages and death benefits.

2. Proper completion of the Personal Tax Credit Return and it's sister, *Form T1213 Request to Reduce Tax Deductions at Source* will help you pay the right amount of tax all year long.

3. Another reason employees overpay their taxes is because they don't diversity their income sources.

4. Employees should discuss the reduction of automobile standby charges with their payroll department.

5. Employees should also check out several tax free benefits:
   - The value of apprentice mechanic's tools paid by the employer,
   - Employer-paid education costs,
   - Financial counseling for re-employment or retirement,
   - Up to $500 in non-cash gifts,

- Gifts containing corporate logos,
- Reimbursements of $15,000 of losses on the sale of an employee's home, if the employer required the move, plus one half of any excess up to the amount of the loss,
- Premiums paid for private health insurance premiums.

6. Several opportunities exist to buy back and claim deductions for past contributions under Registered Pension Plans.

7. Note that pension adjustments resulting from contributions to Registered Pension Plans at work will limit the deduction available to the taxpayer for RRSP purposes.

8. When an employer-provided loan is used to acquire income-producing investments, the amount of the interest benefit shown on the T4 will be deductible as a carrying charge.

9. When an employer-provided loan is forgiven, however, or settled for an amount less than the principal outstanding, the forgiven amount must be included in the taxpayer's income.

10. Employee stock options offer an excellent way to tap into equity and earn tax-deferred capital.

11. Commissioned salespeople and long distance truckers may each claim meal expenses, but they will be subject to restrictions.

12. Auto expense cost and allowances have a variety of tax consequences and must be supported by an auto log to be deductible.

13. Taxpayers who acquire luxury or "passenger vehicles" will be subject to restrictions on their capital cost, leasing and interest expenses.

14. Home office expenses may be deductible, however, they may not be used to create a loss from employment or business income. Excess expenses may be carried forward, though, to offset future income.

15. The GST rebate is often missed by those who claim professional or union dues on Line 212 of the tax return or employment expenses on Line 229. If so, adjust tax returns for the previous 10 year period.

16. Lucrative moving expenses may be claimed by those who transfer to new work locations.

17. Be sure to plan for tax-wise terminations—tax on severance packages can often be minimized.

18. In tough times, avoid paying a clawback of Employment Insurance benefits (this happens when net income exceeds $48,750) if you can use an RRSP contribution to reduce income. Seasonal high income construction workers or executives who receive a pink slip late in the year are especially susceptible to this situation.

NOW PUT MORE MONEY IN YOUR POCKET ALL YEAR LONG...

PERSPECTIVE

We started this chapter by telling you the average tax refund hovers around the $1,200 a year mark or about $100 a month. When you choose to invest that money into a tax-assisted plan like an RRSP instead you'll not only accumulate $1,200 in capital, but you'll save on your taxes too—just under $400 if your taxable income is around $35,000 . . .just over $500 if your income is around $75,000, depending on where you live.

A 33% to 43% after-tax return on your investment is not bad these days.

Never overpay your taxes. . .*pay yourself first.* Use another method of forced savings. Instruct your employer to deposit $50 per pay cheque into your RRSP account. Make this happen by:

- Reducing your withholding taxes immediately. Fill out the *TD1 Tax Credit Return* your employer gives you at the start of each year properly.

- Completing *Form T1213 Request to Reduce Tax Deductions at Source,* if you're going to make a direct deposit to your RRSP through your payroll—or if you will have significant charitable donations, child care expenses, tax deductible alimony payments, deductible employment expenses, interest or carrying charges on investment loans, or proprietorship or rental property losses.

- Investing your refund following sound money management rules:
  - Think about your RRSP as your first investment. Then use those tax savings to,
  - Eliminate non-deductible debt (like credit cards) with your tax refund,
  - Pay down your non-deductible mortgage interest,
  - Open a non-registered savings account to start accumulating a diverse income stream from interest, dividends, real estate investments or capital gains.

We'll show you how in the next several chapters. . .

CHAPTER THREE

ESSENTIAL TAX FACTS
FOR NEW INVESTORS

In the New Millennium, everyone is a new investor. If you really want to be a millionaire some day, you'll need the discipline to start saving now and in the process, get a grip on your largest lifetime expense—your taxes. Make tax efficiency a goal in generating investment income by learning how to:

- Save the first, not the last dollar
- Invest now to accumulate the most
- Create new capital: make your RRSP contribution
- Avoid RRSP contribution bloopers
- Manage tax pre-paid investments
- Calculate marginal tax rates on investment income
- Know the basic rules in reporting interest income
- Understand tax consequences of asset dispositions
- Report interest from T-bills and bonds properly
- Maximize tax opportunities with dividends
- Manage mutual and segregated fund transactions with savvy
- Know tax rules behind your revenue properties
- Avoid Attribution Rules on family income splitting
- Maximize tax-preferred education savings
- Deduct professional fees, interest & carrying charges
- Minimize quarterly instalment payment requirements

Saving the first, not the last dollar

For many people, the filing of their tax return is the most significant financial transaction of the year. It's deadline driven, comes with the threat of rather awesome consequences for non-compliance, and forces you to take an annual glance at your financial affairs—a kind of "financial physical", if you will.

Working and saving money is all the more meaningful when you apply all available tax preferences to basic money management techniques. That is, when you combine the time value of money with tax-efficient investing, family income splitting and tax cost averaging, you'll multiply your economic efforts and accumulate more wealth.

What do we mean by "time value of money"? The concept is simple: a dollar in your pocket today is more valuable than a dollar to be received in the future. When you compute present value, you calculate what your cash flow in the future will be worth in today's dollars. When you calculate future value, you determine how large an investment today will grow to be in the future.

It is important to understand both the present and future value of every dollar you earn. You can make today's dollar work for you immediately by investing it. . .but only if it is in your possession in the first place. That's why you need to plan to take more of the first dollars you make by being vigilant about tax overpayments at source. In a perfect world, each extra dollar should then be invested with a view to cutting taxes even further now, and all year long!

Too good to be true? Not at all—it's possible to have your cake and eat it to, when it comes to tax-efficient capital accumulation. But you've just got to believe. . .in the discipline of saving your money. You can do it! Accumulating capital is so motivating, when you "get the numbers".

Invest now to accumulate the most

The potential value of today's investable assets over time is often projected by analyzing the powerful combination of investment time to maturity, rates of return, inflation rates and tax efficient income structure. Consider these facts:

Unless you write savings directly into your budget, you likely won't have any. It doesn't have to be much, just be sure you write it in. Start with a reasonable goal. . .$1000 a year. That's $2.74 cents a day, or $19.23 a week, or $83.33 a month. How much money will you have if you save $2.75, every day until you retire?

Age Today	Years to Age 65	Capital Saved
25	40	$40,150
35	30	$30,113
45	20	$20,075

Now consider what a difference starting early can make. The following show the investment of $1000 a year at an annual compounding rate of 10%:

A. Invests $1,000 a year starting at age 20		B. Invest $1,000 a year starting at age 30	
Age	Accumulations	Age	Accumulations
20	$ 1,000	20	nil
30	$ 17,531	30	$ 1,000
40	$ 45,470	40	$18,531
50	$117,939	50	$64,003
Total Capital Invested: $10,000		Total Capital Invested: $21,000	

Even though Investor A invested less than half as much capital, s/he ends up with over twice as much capital at the end of a 40 year period. It pays to save first, party later.

Finally, add the power of tax sheltering to your $1000 at an annual compounding rate of 10%, and the results are even more astounding:

Years	Value of Investment Outside RRSP Principle in After Tax Dollars: $720 Assuming a 28% tax rate	Value of an Investment inside RRSP, Principle in Pre-Tax Dollars: $1,000
10	$ 13,342	$ 18,531
20	$ 46,082	$ 64,003
30	$130,999	$ 181,943
40	$351,253	$ 487,852

Remember to take into account that, along the way, your RRSP contribution has done so much more than earn tax sheltered income. It has actually created new capital for you by decreasing your taxes payable and in some cases, increasing social benefits—often with combined marginal tax benefit of well over 50%. That's a great return for your money. It's also a hedge against inflation.

Inflation erodes the purchasing power of your dollar. At an inflation rate of 2%, the future value of $1.00 today will be 67 cents in 20 years. That means the purchasing power of $500,000 in savings will be about $334,000. Yikes! You'll need to protect every dollar you earn even more. . .and one way to do this is by looking out for the best real rates of return over time, taking into account both inflation and taxes. Ask your financial advisors about this.

So, if you really want to be a millionaire some day, you'll start saving now and in the process, get a grip on your largest lifetime expense—your taxes. Make that happen by prioritizing how you use your most important productivity tools—time and money:

- Don't overpay taxes at source (withholding or instalment)
- Always make your RRSP contribution.
- Keep an emergency fund at hand in a non-registered account.
- Look for the best rates of return after inflation and taxes.
- Keep credit card balances down (don't give away high rates of return to your credit card company especially since they are generally not tax deductible).
- Invest with tax efficiency in your non-registered investment accounts.

Create new capital: make your RRSP contribution

So you've bought into the concept of tax-efficient capital accumulation! Then let's hone your technical knowledge of investment choices a little further. If you are a new investor, the first thing you're likely to be asked when you're opening a savings account is this: will you be opening a registered or non-registered account with us?

Investments held in a "registered account" will have the following characteristics:

- Investment income earned by the principal will be tax deferred until withdrawal. This allows capital to compound faster than if tax were paid along the way.

- The principal you invest may produce a tax deduction for the principal invested. The prime example is the Registered Retirement Savings Plans (RRSPs), which is based on your unused RRSP contribution room, as calculated by the CRA. That's great, because new dollars are immediately available for investment purposes through reduced taxation and increased social benefits available through the tax system.

- Another registered investment that produces a tax deduction is the Registered Pension Plan (RPP) which is a company sponsored plan funded by contributions of the employer and employee. Income earned within that plan is also tax deferred.

- Some registered plans don't produce a deduction, but feature tax-sheltered income earning opportunities. These include Registered Education Savings Plans (RESPs), which we will discuss in more detail in the next chapter, and Deferred Profit Sharing Plans (DPSPs).

Essential TAX FACT #64

Your net income on Line 236 of the return will be reduced by your deduction for RPP and RRSP contributions.

- When accumulations within a registered plan are later withdrawn for your use, both principal and earnings are added to income in full.

This is a good thing if you want to claim more non-refundable credits like medical expenses on your own return or transfer certain amounts to your parents' or spouse's return. A low net family income will also increase federal refundable tax credits like the Child Tax Benefit or the GST Credits. It all means more cash for you throughout the year.

Essential TAX FACT #65

When your investment earnings compound on a tax-deferred basis within a registered account, you tap into the most tax efficient way to earn investment income.

When it comes to tax advantages, investing within a registered account essentially enables some double dipping: new dollars are created for investment purposes with your tax deduction, while tax on investment earnings is deferred into the future. That's a great game plan, and it's legal too!

But there is one catch: you will be restricted in the amounts you can sock away in your registered accounts. In the case of the RRSP, your maximum contribution is based on your "unused RRSP contribution room."

Avoid RRSP contribution bloopers

Personal financial independence. That's the goal. . .now what's the time line? You'll achieve your dreams faster if you make it a rule to invest your maximum allowable contribution to an RRSP every year.

Essential TAX FACT #66

The amount you can contribute to an RRSP is based on your "unused RRSP contribution room". This figure can be found on your Notice of Assessment or Reassessment.

Essential TAX FACT #67

You must file a tax return to create unused RRSP contribution room.

Unused RRSP contribution room is a notional account the CRA sets up for you when you file a tax return and report the required "earned income" for RRSP contribution purposes. Earned income is mostly income from actively-earned sources, like employment and self employment but can include net rental income, CPP disability pensions and taxable alimony payments received.

Filing a return can be to your benefit, even if you are not taxable. Moms who work part-time, children with modelling careers, teenagers who work as babysitters or retirees who work part-time as lawn care specialists—all should file a return to build RRSP contribution room.

Why? By reducing net income with an RRSP deduction, family net income will be decreased for the purposes of claiming refundable tax credits. Lowered net incomes might also enable the transfer of certain provisions—like tuition and education amounts—between family members.

So just how much can you contribute? RRSP contribution room is the lesser of:

- 18% of earned income from the prior tax year minus any net "Pension Adjustment" (PA) for the current year, and

- the maximum RRSP "deduction limit" for the current year minus any net Pension Adjustments for the current year.

Let's define some of those terms. The "Pension Adjustment" is a measure of benefits the taxpayer received as a member of another pension plan at work, such as an RPP (Registered Pension Plan) or DPSP (Deferred Profit Sharing Plan).

The RRSP "deduction limit" has been increasing of late:

2004—$15,500
2005—$16,500
2006—$18,000

CRA provides a worksheet for calculating RRSP contribution room in its Guide: *RRSPs and Other Registered Plans for Retirement.* You might want to check this out. But usually figuring out how much you can contribute begins with looking for your Unused Contribution Room on your Notice of Assessment or Reassessment from the CRA.

The RRSP deduction is recorded on Schedule 7 and from there on Line 208 of the tax return. This deduction can therefore consist of:

- RRSP contributions made in prior years and not deducted or refunded

- RRSP contributions made in the tax year

- RRSP contributions made in the first 60 days after the end of the tax year

Essential TAX FACT #68

If you don't make the full allowable contribution to your RRSP, the unused RRSP contribution room may be carried forward for use in the future.

Essential TAX FACT #69

Besides the requirement for unused RRSP contribution room, a taxpayer must be under 70 years of age to contribute to an RRSP. . unless there is a younger spouse.

Age Eligibility. Note that there is no lower age limit for contributing to an RRSP. As long as CRA has the unused RRSP contribution room recorded, even a 6 year old can make a contribution. But, RRSPs must be collapsed by the end of the year in which the taxpayer turns 69.

Spousal RRSPs. Taxpayers may contribute to their own RRSPs based on available RRSP contribution room, but may also contribute some or all of the amounts to a spousal RRSP. This provides for income splitting advantages on retirement and can help an age-ineligible taxpayer prolong the ability to use an RRSP deduction. Spousal RRSPs are not subject to the Attribution Rules, that is, you can gift money to your spouse's RRSP and have the resulting income taxed in the spouse's hands. . .but there is a catch.

Essential
TAX FACT #70

Withdrawals from a spousal RRSP will be taxed in the contributor's hands if the money is withdrawn within 3 years of the last spousal RRSP contribution.

John, for example, has been making his own and spousal RRSP contributions every year to equalize pension accumulations. If his wife Sofi withdraws money from the spousal RRSP within three years of the last spousal RRSP contribution by John, the withdrawal will be taxed in John's hands.

Essential
TAX FACT #71

Those taxpayers who are "age ineligible" may still contribute to a spousal RRSP, based on their own RRSP contribution room, if their spouse is under 69 years old.

An exception to this rule occurs when the spousal RRSP accumulations are transferred into a Registered Retirement Income Fund or RRIF. (See next chapter for more details in creating a pension from your RRSP accumulations). In that case only the amounts in excess of the minimum amount you are required to withdraw will be taxed in the hands of the contributor to the spousal RRSP.

Essential
TAX FACT #72

If you are 18 or over, an "over contribution" can be made to your RRSP—up to a maximum of $2000.

If John in our example above, had turned 70 this year, he could no longer contribute to his own RRSP even though he still has unused RRSP contribution room of $5000. His wife Sofi is 65, though. John can choose to make a spousal RRSP contribution, thereby depositing the money into Sofi's RRSP. He can then take the deduction on his return.

In addition, certain "tax free rollovers" of qualifying receipts into an RRSP will also be allowed. These will be discussed in Chapter 4.

The point of all of this is of course to claim your RRSP deduction on Line 208 of the return. But, what happens if you don't need the tax deduction to reduce income? Can you use it next year?

Consider this example: Terry is an MBA student who is not taxable, but who maximizes his RRSP contribution room every year. He knows that he does not need to take the tax deduction, but can save his "unused RRSP contributions" for next year, when he will be working and earning $80,000. He will get a bigger bang for his RRSP buck that way.

Essential TAX FACT #73

Any amounts contributed in the year and not deducted are considered to be "unused RRSP contributions." These amounts may be carried forward and deducted in future years if this is more advantageous for the taxpayer to do so.

It can really pay off in big way to make your RRSP contribution when your marginal tax advantage is greatest. . .that should take into account the value of social benefits you will qualify for, too .

Consider another example: Sam is a single father with three children. He earns $45,000 at his job as a security officer and pays $6,000 per year in child care. Net Income is therefore $39,000, putting Alex in clawback zone for the Child Tax Benefit. This means his benefits will be reduced because he has exceeded pre-set income thresholds. If he can contribute to an RRSP he will be able to increase his Child Tax Benefit and reduce his taxes, too.

Ask your tax advisor to compute your marginal tax advantages, or use your tax software to do "what if" scenarios yourself. . .what if I contributed $1000, $5000, $10,000 and so on.

Essential TAX FACT #74

When RRSP contributions are made by transferring capital property into the account, the taxpayer is deemed to have disposed of the capital asset at the time of the transfer.

But suppose you just don't have any new money to contribute to an RRSP? Here's more good news: RRSP contributions may be made in cash or in kind. That is, a taxpayer may transfer an eligible investment from his non-registered investments to his RRSP and may claim a deduction for the fair market value of the asset at the time of the transfer.

If the fair market value at the time of the transfer is higher than the cost of the asset to the taxpayer, then the taxpayer will have to report the capital gain in his income for the year.

However, here's a trap: if the fair market value of the asset is less than the taxpayer's cost, then the loss will be deemed to be nil. That is, it will not be claimable.

Therefore, if the taxpayer wishes to transfer an asset, which has decreased in value, to his RRSP in order to create a tax deduction, it's best to sell the asset, contribute the proceeds to his RRSP and then have the RRSP repurchase the asset. This method will allow the taxpayer to deduct the capital loss on his tax return.

The following are examples of qualifying investments in an RRSP:

- publicly traded shares and shares of public corporations
- shares of small business corporations (as long as the annuitant is not a connected shareholder)
- shares of venture capital corporations
- bonds, debentures, notes, mortgages, or similar obligations of, or guaranteed by, the Government of Canada (e.g., Canada Savings Bonds) or of a province, municipality or Crown corporation
- guaranteed investment certificates issued by a Canadian trust company
- bonds, debentures, notes or similar obligations issued by a corporation listed on a prescribed stock exchange in or outside of Canada
- "stripped bonds"
- A mortgage, or an interest therein, in respect of real property situated in Canada.
- a mutual fund trust
- Royalty or partnership units listed on a prescribed stock exchange in Canada.

Essential TAX FACT #75

If an RRSP holds more than 30% of the book value of its assets in foreign investments it will be subject to a penalty tax.

An exception to these foreign content restrictions occurs when the RRSP holds small business investments. In that case, the foreign content may be as high as 50% without attracting a penalty tax. On top of the 30% limit, the RRSP may hold $3 of foreign investments for each dollar invested in qualifying small business properties to a maximum of 20%.

Those foreign content rules kick in for each individual RRSP held by the taxpayer, not on the accumulated RRSP investments, so caution must be exercised to ensure that each RRSP remains within its foreign content limitations.

Now that your have maxed your RRSP advantages, let's work on your next level of tax efficient investment options: contributions to non-registered savings accounts.

Essential TAX FACT #76

The more after-tax dollars you have to invest today, the wealthier you'll be in the future.

Manage tax pre-paid investments

When you earn income from your investments, you can arrange your affairs within the framework of the law to:

- shelter your income from tax in the present
- defer taxation of your income into the future
- earn the types of income which attract the least amount of tax
- take advantage of our progressive tax system by splitting income with other family members

To do this, you must understand when investment earnings are "realized" or reportable for tax purposes, and that all income sources are not taxed alike. To begin, there are two broad classifications of income of your investment activities which are important to note:

- Income from Business or Property
- Capital gains and losses

Essential TAX FACT #77

Income from a business or property specifically does not include capital gains or losses from the disposition of such property.

Income from property includes interest, dividends, rent and royalties. The amounts are claimed on Schedule 4 of the tax return, or in the case of rental properties, a *Statement of Rental Income* (Form T776).

Your capital transactions are reported separately on Schedule 3 – *Statement of Capital Gains and Losses,* and only at the time of disposition.

Income from property vs. income from a business. Income from business and property are discussed together in the Income Tax Act and therefore are subject to many of the same general rules, when it comes to income reporting and expense deductibility.

**Essential
TAX FACT #78**

Canada's "self assessment" system puts the onus of proof on you the taxpayer, to keep accurate account of gross revenues earned or earnable in the future, and all expenses incurred to arrive at both gross and net income.

A business, for example, is defined as: a "profession, calling, trade, manufacture or undertaking of any kind whatever, and except for certain capital properties, an adventure or concern in the nature of trade." Specifically this definition does not include an office or employment, income from property or capital gains or losses. There must also be a *reasonable expectation of profit,* on an annual and cumulative basis over the ownership period. That is, it must be shown that expenses have been incurred to earn gross revenues that result in a reasonable expectation of profit over time.

When you file your return, you should also know about several key restrictions on your expenses:

- *General limitation on expense deductibility:* No tax deduction is ever allowed except to the extent that it is reasonable in the circumstances.

- *Personal and living expenses.* No deduction is allowed for personal or living expenses unless you incur traveling expenses while away from home in carrying on business. To deal with "mixed use expenditures" a proration is required to remove any personal component of the cost.

- *Capital outlays or loss.* Outlays, loss or replacement of capital, a payment on account of capital or an allowance in respect of depreciation, obsolescence or depletion cannot be claimed as deductions. However, the capital gain or loss reported on the disposition of such capital may be adjusted.

- *Limitation for exempt income.* No deduction will be allowed when expenses are incurred to earn exempt income.

- *Limit on interest and property tax.* Interest or property taxes paid on vacant land held for resale or development is not deductible except if it is held in the course of a business or for the primary purpose of gaining or producing income from the land.

- *Limits on RRSP Contributions.* Because of its passive nature, income from property is not included in the computation of "earned income" for RRSP contribution purposes. However, net income earned from a business or a rental property will qualify as RRSP earned income.

- *Reporting of Income from Property.* Income from property is reported as received or receivable on a calendar year basis. The calendar year is also used to report income received or receivable by unincorporated businesses, although an election to use a fiscal year may be available in the case of the active business enterprise.

- *Reporting of Accrued Interest income.* On investment contracts acquired after 1989, interest is considered to accrue for tax purposes on the contract's anniversary date, and this accrued interest must be reported annually on the return. This is required whether or not the taxpayer actually receives the interest in the year (which likely will not be the case on compounding investments.)

- *No CPP Contributions on Income from Property.* Neither investment income or net rental income qualifies for the purposes of making CPP contributions.

Now here's the tax skinny on your investment income sources:

- **Interest income:** This is the least efficient investment income source. The full amount of accrued income must be reported annually—so you pay tax on compounding earnings before you receive them. For this reason, taxpayers often plan to earn interest income inside registered accounts.

- **Dividends:** Dividends are the after-tax distributions of profit from a corporation. Dividends from taxable Canadian corporations are "grossed up" for tax purposes on the individual return by 25% to put them on a pre-tax basis, then the dividend tax credit of 13 1/3% of the grossed up dividend provides tax relief on Schedule 1 of your return. As a result, dividends are often more tax efficient, except when they decrease refundable or non-refundable tax credits and increase clawbacks by artificially increasing your net income on line 236.

- **Rents:** It is net rental income—gross rents less operating costs and capital cost allowances—that is reported for tax purposes. Net rental earnings qualify for RRSP earned income purposes and can be reduced to zero with a capital cost allowance claim. However, rental loss deductibility can be restricted in some cases.

- **Royalties:** It is possible to set off some resource royalty income with a resource allowance. Royalties from publishing ventures are reported as business income.

- **Capital gains or losses:** Although not considered to be income from property, you should know that a capital gain is not "realized" for tax purposes until there is an actual or deemed disposition, and then only 50% of the gain or loss is taxable. More on this in the next chapter.

Calculate marginal tax rates on investment income

If you are going to manage your capital accumulations, you need to know your marginal tax rates on your investments. These were briefly defined in Chapter 1 of this book.

**Essential
TAX FACT #79**

The marginal tax rate is the rate of tax paid on the next dollar earned or the next dollar spent. As income sources can be reported differently for tax purposes, you need to understand income source, income level and rates of taxes applied to calculate this.

To be completely accurate, marginal tax rates should take into account the effect of the next dollar of income on refundable tax credits and of course the provincial taxes. The most effective way to determine the marginal tax rate is to calculate the income taxes payable on the return, plus refundable credits, and then add $100 of the type of income that will next be earned. Note the new taxes payable plus the revised amount of refundable credits receivable. The difference is the marginal tax rate as a percentage.

The marginal tax rate will differ depending on your source of income, as well as your income level. Capital gains attract one-half of the marginal tax rate for ordinary income, for example. The MTR for dividend income is not as easily calculated, as the dividend tax credit rate varies by province, but dividends generally attract a lower rate than interest or ordinary income, but a higher one than capital gains.

The MTR is an effective tool in comparing the after-tax rate of return on different investment types as well as calculating the return on investments which reduce taxable income, such as RRSP contributions.

Visit www.knowledgebureau.com for a summary of marginal tax rates on income sources.

Know the basic rules for reporting interest income

A debt obligation can generally be defined as an investment contract between borrower and a lender to repay the amount invested by the lender plus interest, which can often accrue on a compounding basis (that is, interest is reinvested rather than paid out to the investor during the term of the contract). Such contracts can take on a variety of formats. For example:

- A Guaranteed Investment Certificate which features a fixed interest rate for a term spanning generally one to five years.
- A Canada Savings Bond
- A treasury bill or zero coupon bond stipulates no interest and is acquired at a discount to its maturity value.
- A strip bond or coupon pays interest, but at a disproportionate amount relative to the underlying principal.
- A Guaranteed Investment Certificate offering interest rates that rise as time goes on. These are also known as deferred interest obligations.
- An income bond or debenture that is linked to a corporation's profit or cash flow
- An indexed debt obligation instrument that is linked to inflation rates, for example Government of Canada Real Return Bonds.

Interest reporting follows two basic tax rules:

1. When interest is actually received or receivable (as is the case from regular bonds) you must report the interest in the taxation year received or receivable.
2. In the case of compounding investments (that is interest is reinvested

rather than paid out so that you can earn interest on interest during the term of the investment), you must report all interest income that accrues in the tax year to the bonds' anniversary date. That's right, you pay tax first, receive income later in the case of your multi-year compounding investments. One could say it's the government which benefits from the time value of money in this case.

The issue date is important—reporting stems from there rather than date of ownership for tax reporting purposes. Also, because of the annual reporting rules, which apply to investments acquired after 1989, an issue date in November of one year, for example, does not require interest reporting until the following year. In other words, the accrual of interest for the period November to December 31 is not required.

You should be aware that for investment acquired in the period 1981 up to and including 1989, a three year reporting cycle was required, but the taxpayer could switch to annual accrual reporting if desired.

Interest income reporting is often obvious: you will receive a T5, T3 or T600 slip, depending on the investment. Interest received or accrued each year must be reported as investment income on *Schedule 4 – Statement of Investment Income*, and Line 121 of the tax return.

Note: because you may not have received a slip, you will not be excused from reporting interest income.

Canada Savings Bonds. Although the name implies that these debt obligations are bonds, Canada Savings Bonds do not have many of the characteristics of other bonds. They are issued by the Government of Canada, are non-marketable and redeemable on demand. After the first three months, they will pay interest up to the end of the month prior to cashing; otherwise interest is paid on November 1 each year, in the case of regular bond holders. Compound bonds are also available.

Things get a little trickier when investment contracts have unique features:

- they may be non-interest bearing and sold at a discount to their maturity value
- the interest rates paid account for inflation over time
- interest is higher as the term progresses or
- interest payments depend on the debtor's cash flows or profits.
- where the instrument is transferred before the end of the term, a reconciliation of interest earnings must take place.

Here are some examples:

Regular government or corporate bonds can also be called "coupon bonds" which pay a stated rate of interest. If the stated interest rate earned is from a Canadian source it will be reported on a T5 slip and entered on the tax return in the calendar year received in the normal manner. If from a foreign source, interest is reported annually in Canadian funds on Schedule 4 and may qualify for a foreign tax credit if taxes have been withheld at source in the foreign country.

Zero coupon bonds, strip coupons or T-Bills (Treasury Bills) feature no stated interest rate. You will need to know how to report the interest income that is considered to be accruing.

Further complications arise when the bond or coupon is sold before maturity. In that case, the new investor in the bond will receive interest on the next payment date, as usual, even though some of the interest may have accrued prior to the purchase. An adjustment must be made to ensure each bond owner reports the correct

Essential TAX FACT #83

Over time, fluctuations in the rate of interest will affect the value of bonds. In general when interest rates rise, the value of a bond or debenture paying a fixed rate of interest will decrease, and vice versa. In those cases, a capital gain or loss may result upon disposition.

amount of interest up to the date ownership change. In addition, a capital gain or loss might arise on the disposition.

Understand tax consequences of asset dispositions

Essential TAX FACT #84

A capital gain (or loss) occurs when an income-producing asset is disposed of for an amount that exceeds (or is less than) its original cost on acquisition plus certain adjustments.

To understand the tax consequences upon disposition of an income-producing asset, a short lesson in capital gains or losses is required. We will be discussing capital acquisitions and dispositions in more depth in the next chapter on Wealth Preservation, but by way of introduction, you should know the following basic terms.

In a mathematical equation, a capital gain (or loss) looks like this:

Capital Gain (or Loss) = **Proceeds of Disposition less**
Adjusted Cost Base less
Outlays and Expenses Incurred

The *proceeds of disposition* can be the actual sales price received less outlays and expenses like broker's commissions. But proceeds can also be a "deemed" amount (the fair market value, for example) in cases where there is a taxable disposition but no money changes hands—death, transfer or property or emigration, for example.

The *adjusted cost base* is based on the cost of an income-producing asset, when acquired. This could be a cash outlay, or in the case of acquisition by way of a transfer due to gift, inheritance, etc., the fair market value is used. However, the ACB may also be increased or decreased by certain adjustments: the cost of improvements to the asset, for example, or in the case of our bond topic, certain interest adjustments.

For example, Jonas buys shares for $100 plus $10 commission and sells them six months later for $200 less $20 commission.

- The "Adjusted Cost Base" of the shares is $110 (price paid, including commissions).
- The "Proceeds of Disposition" are $200.

- The $20 commission on sale is an "outlay and expense" of sale.
- The "Capital Gain" is $200 - $110 - $20 = **$70**.

Report interest from T-Bills and bonds properly

So now, back to interest-bearing investments. How do you report income, when there is an interest component and you later sell the asset for more than its cost base? Some illustrations follow:

Treasury Bills. These are short-term government debt obligations, generally available in three, six or twelve month terms. If the T-bill's term exceeds one year, the normal annual interest accrual rules would apply.

T-Bills are similar to strip bonds (discussed below) because they are acquired at a discount to their maturity value and have no stated interest rate. On maturity you will usually receive their "par" value, which will include the accrued interest amount. This is generally reported on a T5008 slip. If you sell the T-Bill before maturity, a capital gain or loss could result. This is how you would calculate the tax consequences:

1. Calculate the interest that has accrued in the period of ownership. Report this as interest income on the tax return.
2. Calculate the proceeds of disposition less the interest accrued.
3. Reduce this figure by the adjusted cost base
4. Subtract any outlays and expenses, such as brokerage fees
5. The result is the capital gain or loss.

For example, a T-Bill with a face value of $10,000 is acquired for $9600 and a brokerage fee of $50 is paid to do so. The bill was disposed of before end of term for $9900, at which time a brokerage fee of $75 was paid. It had been held for 188 days.

1. Interest to be reported = $10,000 − 9600 = $300 x 188/365 = $154.52. The brokerage fee of $50 is claimed as a carrying charge on Line 221.
2. Calculate Adjusted Cost Base: $9600 + $154.52 + $50 = $9804.52
3. Capital Gain on Disposition: $20.48, calculated as follows: Proceeds of Disposition = $9900 less ACB $9804.52 less Outlays and Expenses $75= **$20.48**

Strip Bonds. These are also known as zero-coupon bonds as they do not pay interest during the period of ownership. They are purchased at a discount or present value—and if held over a specific term will yield a future value that is higher. The difference between the present and future value is considered to be the interest paid over the period to maturity. The resulting interest amount must be reported annually on the anniversary date of the bond's issue date each year.

Essential
TAX FACT #85

If a strip bond is sold prior to its maturity date, a capital gain or loss may result. The Adjusted Cost Base (ACB) used in the calculation of the gain or loss will be the original amount paid for the strip bond plus the interest accrued from the date of purchase to the date of disposition.

Here's an example:

The yield rate on a 5 year bond sold at a discount of 20% of the face value is 4.564% [(10,000/8,000) (1/5) - 1] so the interest accrued on the bond would be:

Year	Interest	Value
0		$ 8,000.00
1	$ 365.12	$ 8,365.12
2	$ 381.78	$ 8,746.90
3	$ 399.20	$ 9,146.10
4	$ 417.42	$ 9,563.52
5	$ 436.48	$10,000.00

If the bond sold for $9,000 with three years remaining, the yield to maturity would be 3.5744% [(10,000/9,000)(1/3) – 1] so the interest accrued after the sale to the new owner would be:

Year	Interest	Value
0		$ 9,000.00
1	$ 321.70	$ 9,321.70
2	$ 333.19	$ 9,654.89
3	$ 345.11	$10,000.00

On disposition in mid term, accrued interest is added to the adjusted cost base, outlays and expenses are deducted to compute the capital gain or loss. The adjusted cost base for the new owner is the cost of the property ($9000 in this case).

Indexed Debt Obligations include, in addition to interest paid on the amount invested, a payment (or deduction) on maturity that represents the decrease (or increase) in the purchasing power of the investment during the term of the investment. This additional payment is reported according to the normal annual accrual rules. An adjusting entry in the form of a deduction, may be required in the year of disposition if there has been an over-accrual.

Income Bonds and Income Debentures. A special type of bond or debenture may be issued with terms up to 5 years by corporations that are in financial difficulty and under the control of a receiver or trustee in bankruptcy. A return on such an income bond is paid only if the issuing corporation earns a profit from its operations. Such amounts paid or received by the investor are then treated as a dividend for tax purposes.

Exchanges of Debentures for Securities. When a bond or debenture is exchanged for shares of a corporation, the exchange is not considered to be a disposition for tax purposes, providing that the share is received directly from the corporation which issued it. Therefore there are no tax consequences. This is also true when one debenture is exchanged for another bond or debenture, providing that the principal amount is the same.

Maximize tax opportunities with dividends

A return of the after-tax profits of a corporation to its shareholders is known as a "dividend". Dividends received from Canadian corporations are subject to special rules, as an adjustment must be made to compensate for the taxes already paid by the corporation. To do this, the actual dividends received are grossed up by 25% for personal tax purposes. This increases the taxpayer's net income on Line 236.

This grossed-up dividend amount then qualifies for a Dividend Tax Credit of 13.33%. This is computed on Schedule 1 and reduces federal taxes payable. A separate dividend tax credit calculation is made on the provincial tax forms as well.

Because the dividend "gross up" artificially increases net income, it will reduce refundable or non-refundable tax credits for the taxpayer, such as:

• The Canada Child Tax Benefit

- The GST Credit
- Provincial refundable tax credits
- The Age Amount
- The Spousal Amount
- Amount for Eligible Dependant
- Medical expenses
- Amounts for Other Adult Dependants
- Charitable Donations

It will also negatively affect other financial transactions that are dependent upon the size of net income on the tax return:

- Old Age Security Clawbacks
- Employment Insurance Clawbacks
- Guaranteed Income Supplements
- Provincial per diem rates for nursing homes
- Certain provincial medical/prescription plans.

Therefore income planning around investment options is important, especially for seniors, and should take into account all of the provisions above.

An investor should be aware of the tax consequences of the following types of dividends:

- *Capital Dividends.* Sometimes a shareholder in a private corporation may receive a Capital Dividend. Such dividends are received on a tax-free basis.

  To qualify as a Capital Dividend, the dividend must be paid out of the Capital Dividend Account (CDA) of a private Canadian corporation. This account is set up to store the non-taxable (50%) portion of any capital gains realized by the corporation during its operations, capital dividends received from other corporations, untaxed portions of gains realized on the disposition of eligible capital property, and life insurance proceeds received by the corporation.

- *Capital Gains Dividends.* These are dividends received from a mutual fund company. They are reported on a T5 Slip and Schedule 3. Capital gains dividends are considered to be Capital Gains and not Dividends (that is, they are taxed at 50%, are not grossed up and are not eligible for the dividend tax credit).

- *Stock Dividends.* This type of dividend arises when a corporation decides to issue additional shares to its existing shareholders, instead of paying a cash dividend. Like regular dividends, stock dividends must be included in income, and are subject to the 25% gross-up, and the dividend tax credit. The amount of the dividend is the market value of a single share on the date of issue, multiplied by the number of shares received.

The corporation will issue a T5 slip to the recipient of a dividend in almost all cases.

Income Splitting Opportunities. A special rule allows the transfer of dividends from one spouse to another if by doing so a Spousal Amount is created or increased. The dividend income is left off the lower-income spouse's tax return, in such a case and it is instead reported by the higher-income spouse, who can then use the offsetting dividend tax credit. Note that if this election is made, it must be applied to all dividend income from taxable Canadian corporations. See more on income splitting at the end of this chapter.

Manage mutual and segregated fund transactions with savvy

Mutual funds are such a common investment today, yet few people really understand the tax consequences and the requirement to keep track of the adjusted cost base of their investment.

The term "adjusted cost base" came up earlier in the discussion of bond dispositions. There you could see that this is a critical figure in computing your gains or losses when an investment is disposed of.

Upon acquisition of the fund, it is important to record the cost and number of units acquired for use in calculating the Adjusted Cost Base along the way. Start a spread sheet and record each investment's cost, including commissions and the number of units acquired. The adjusted cost base is divided by the number of units to arrive at the cost per unit.

Example: Units acquired: 1000. Adjusted Cost Base: $10,000. Per unit: $10.00

Tax Treatment of Distributions. Your adjusted cost base and unit costs will likely be adjusted during the holding period of your investment as mutual funds are required to distribute all interest, dividends, other income and net capital gains or losses to their unit holders at least once every year. With the exception of any return of capital, these distributions are taxable. In the year you acquire a mutual fund, you will usually receive a full annual distribution, even if you invested late in the year.

A T3 Slip (from a mutual fund trust) or a T5 Slip (from a mutual fund corporation) will report these distributions in the proper income categories. Rarely is this income received in cash. Rather, it is used to buy more units in the fund and those reinvested amounts are added to the Adjusted Cost Base. Such proper accounting will decrease capital gains (or increase losses) in the future.

Example: The mutual fund in the above example paid $1000 in income distributions in Year 2. The money was reinvested and now the taxpayer has 1080 units.

Units held: 1080 Adjusted Cost Base: $11,000 Per unit $10.19

Switches and Exchanges. In general, when you exchange an investment in one fund for another (e.g. an equity fund to a balanced fund), a taxable disposition is considered to have occurred, with normal taxable consequences. There are no tax consequences when you switch from one class or series to another class or series of funds.

Tax Consequences Upon Disposition of the Units: When you sell or otherwise dispose of a mutual fund, a taxable capital gain or loss may result. Mutual funds are classified as "identical properties" for tax purposes. The average cost of the shares/units must be calculated each time there is a purchase, by dividing total units owned into the adjusted cost of the assets including all reinvested earnings, as illustrated above. This provides you with the cost per unit required to calculate the capital gains or losses on dispositions properly. Please see next chapter for more information on computing capital gains or losses; however, in the meantime, use the following column headings on your spreadsheet to properly track the numbers:

Date	Cost plus commission	Plus reinvested distributions	Less return of capital	Less ACB of units redeemed	Total	Divided by no. of units	ACB per unit

Segregated Funds. A segregated fund is similar to a mutual fund in that it is a pooled investment, however it is established by an insurance company and the funds invested are segregated from the rest of the capital of the company. The main difference between a segregated and a mutual fund is in the guarantee—that is a minimum amount will always be returned to the investor regardless of the performance of the fund over time.

Income that is allocated out to segregated fund unit holders is reported on a T3 Slip, as the insurance company will have set up a trust for the purposes of creating the segregated fund. Dividend income received from the fund will be eligible for the dividend tax credit, interest will be taxed in the normal manner and any foreign taxes paid on foreign income allocations will qualify for the foreign tax credit.

There are many differences between a mutual fund trust and a segregated fund trust.

When income – interest, dividends or capital gains or losses – is distributed as a result of investment performance, it will be received in the hands of the trust, which then allocates the income out on the basis of units to the investors.

> **Essential TAX FACT #88**
>
> Within a segregated fund, the policyholder does not own the units; the segregated fund trust does. Therefore income allocations do not affect the value of the fund.

Such income allocations do not affect the value of the segregated fund. This is not so when a taxpayer receives distributions out of a mutual fund, as these will affect the value of the mutual fund (it will generally go down on the day of distribution).

Another important investment and tax planning feature of segregated funds is that allocations made from such a fund can take into account the length of time the investor has owned the units. When a mutual fund distributes income, all unit holders receive a share of the distributions as of the day of the distribution, even if they have only held the funds for one day. This can generate a large and unwanted tax liability if the unit holder is not aware.

Seg funds also offer maturity and death guarantees on the capital invested and specifically, reset guarantees—which is the ability to lock in market gains. This can be 75 to 100% of the amount invested, which will be returned to the taxpayer on death or maturity.

Depending on the insurer, a reset can be initiated by the investor two to four times per year. The guaranteed period on maturity is usually 10 years after the policy is purchased, or after the reset. There are no tax consequences at the time the accrued gains in the investment are locked in by way of reset. This can be a very attractive feature of this investment type.

Guarantee at Maturity. If at maturity the value of the fund has dropped, the insurer must top up the fund by contributing additional assets to bring the value up to the guaranteed amount. There are no tax implications at the time of top up. However, there will be when the taxpayer disposes of the fund. This will be the difference between the ACB (which includes allocations of income over time) and the proceeds received.

Guarantee at Death. The policyholder is deemed to have disposed of the contract at its Fair Market Value at time of deemed disposition—death or emigration for example. If the value of the assets in the fund increases, the gain will be taxable to the policyholder when the policy matures or to his estate if the policy owner dies. If the value of the assets in the fund decreases, the taxpayer is deemed to have acquired additional notional units in the fund so that no gain is incurred even though the taxpayer receives more than the value of the notional units. A capital loss may occur if the guaranteed value is less than 100% of the investment.

Foreign Content Rules. After 1997 there are foreign content limits to investments in segregated funds within an RRSP or RRIF. The same foreign content limits must be observed; based on the ACB of the fund. See Registered Retirement Savings Plan (RRSP) for a discussion of foreign content rules.

Know tax rules behind your revenue properties

The real estate market has been hot in many areas of Canada of late, and many have invested in property to get a lift out of their investment dollar. If that investment is in a principal residence, a tax free gain on the sale of your home is possible. This is so even if you earn income from that tax exempt residence—by renting out a room or rooms, for example, or by running a business from your home. We'll dig deeper into the tax consequences of primary and secondary residences or rental properties in the next chapter, but our mandate here is to discuss revenue properties held for investment purposes.

Those who collect rental income from a property rented to tenants will have tax consequences in operating the property and usually upon the disposition of the property as well.

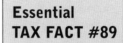

Essential TAX FACT #89

One tax exempt principal residence can be owned per household.

In the first year, it is important to set up tax reporting requirements for a revenue property properly:

- *A Statement of Rental Income* (Form T776) must be completed
- Income and expenses will be reported on a calendar year basis and in general the cash basis of accounting will be used, even though in theory landlords are to use the accrual method of reporting income and expenses as is usual practice with income from businesses.
- Gross rental income must be reported. It is best to open a separate bank account to keep this in, and amounts charged must be at fair rental value.
- Damage deposits must also be reported as income. They will be deducted as expenses when returned to the client.
- Advance payments of rent can be included in income according to the years they relate to.
- Lease cancellation payments received by you are income to you.
- In order to deduct operating expenses from rental income, there must be a reasonable expectation of profit on an annual basis, and, if proposed new rules are passed, over the "profitability" or ownership period.
- Fully deductible operating expenses include maintenance, repairs, supplies, interest, taxes.
- Partially deductible expenses could include the business portion of auto expenses and meal and entertainment expenses incurred.
- Expenditures for asset acquisition or improvement cannot be deducted in full. Rather Capital Cost Allowance (CCA) schedules must be set up to account for the expense of depreciation. In the first year, this deduction must be adjusted for the short fiscal year in which the property was owned.

- As land is not a depreciable asset, it is necessary to separate the cost of land and buildings on the CCA schedule.

- CCA is always taken at the taxpayer's option. It is possible to forego making the claim at all in one year to preserve it for the future, or to account for the fact that the asset is really appreciating—not depreciating in value. A rental loss cannot be created or increased with a CCA claim. CCA classes and rates are discussed in more detail in Chapter 5.

- Not deductible are any expenses that relate to personal living expenses of the owner, or any expenses that relate to the cost of the land or principal portions of loans taken to acquire or maintain the property.

**Essential
TAX FACT #90**

Rentals to family members can be tricky.

When a taxpayer rents a portion of his or her home to a family member for a nominal rent the taxpayer may not claim a rental loss, as there is no reasonable expectation of profit. In this case, the taxpayer need not include the rent in income.

Most expenses incurred to earn rental income will be deductible in the year paid. Expenses must be matched to the rental income. So, if the taxpayer pays insurance in advance, for example, only that portion of the insurance that relates to the rental period may be deducted. Also, if the only way to reap financial benefits from the ownership or the property is through capital appreciation on its sale, there is no profit motive and operating expenses like interest costs cannot be used to increase or create a loss.

Deductible Expenses: Common deductible operating expenses include:

Advertising – Amounts paid to advertise the availability of the rental property
Capital Cost Allowance – Special and important rules apply regarding restorations improvements:

**Essential
TAX FACT #91**

If an expenditure extends the useful life of the property or improves upon the original condition of the property, then the expenditure is capital in nature.

Improvements that extend the useful life of the property (new roof, new fence or new carpeting for example) must be listed on the Capital Cost Allowance schedule, resulting in only a portion of the expenditure being deductible on the CCA rules. On the other hand, a *repair* that returns the property to its original state, such as replacing a piece of the carpet is a current expense, which is 100% deductible.

Condominium fees applicable to the period when the rental condo was available for rent may be deducted.

Insurance – If the insurance prepaid for future years, claim only the portion that applies to the rental year.

Landscaping costs may be deducted in the year paid.

Lease cancellation payments by landlord – deduct that portion of the payment you have made as landlord to the person who leased the property from you according to the amount that relates to the period of the cancelled lease in each year. That is, you will need to deduct these amounts over the term of the lease including renewal periods. In the case of dispositions at arm's length, a final amount may be deducted, but based on the current capital gains inclusion rate (50%). The full amount of the lease cancellation payment may be deducted if the building was considered to be inventory rather than capital property upon its sale.

Legal, Accounting and Other Professional Fees – There are unique rules to consider in deducting fees paid to professionals:

- Legal fees to prepare leases or to collect rent are deductible.
- Legal fees to acquire the property form part of the cost of the property.
- Legal fees on disposition are outlays and expenses which will reduce any capital gains on the sale.
- Accounting fees to prepare statements, keep books, or prepare the tax return are deductible.

Maintenance and Repairs – Costs of regular maintenance and minor repairs are deductible. For major repairs, it must be determined if the cost is a current expense or capital in nature.

Management and Administration Fees – If the taxpayer paid a third party to manage or otherwise look after some aspect of the rental, the amount paid is deductible. Note that if a caretaker is given a suite in an apartment block as compensation for caregiving, a T4 Slip must be issued to report the fair market value of the suite as employment income.

Mortgage Interest – Interest on a mortgage to purchase the property plus any interest on additional loans to improve the rental property may be deducted, provided you can show there is a reasonable expectation of profit from the revenue property. Note:

- If an additional mortgage is taken out against the equity in the property and the proceeds are used for some other purpose, the mortgage interest is not deductible as a rental expense, but may be deductible as carrying charges.

- Other charges relating to acquisition of a mortgage (banking fees, for example) are not deductible in the year paid, but can be amortized over a five-year period starting at the time they were incurred.

- If the interest costs relate to the acquisition of depreciable property, the taxpayer may elect to add the interest to the capital cost of the asset rather than deduct it in the year paid.

Motor Vehicle Expenses – Travelling expenses are generally considered to be personal living expenses of the landlord. If the taxpayer owns only one rental property, then motor vehicle expenses to collect rent are not deductible. However, if the taxpayer personally travels to make repairs to the property, then the cost of transporting tools and materials to the property may be deducted.

Essential TAX FACT #93

If the taxpayer owns rental properties at two or more sites away from the taxpayer's place of residence, CRA will allow motor vehicle costs to collect rent, supervise repairs or otherwise manage the properties.

Office and Office Supplies – office and other supplies used up in the pursuit of rental income are deductible as are home office expenses in situations where the landlord uses the office to keep books or serve tenants.

Property Taxes – These are deductible for the rental units.

Renovations for the Disabled – Costs incurred to make the rental property accessible to individuals with a mobility impairment may be fully deducted.

Travel Costs – The same rules apply here as for motor vehicle costs. Also travel costs to supervise a revenue property do no include the cost of accommodation, which CRA considers to be a personal expense.

Utilities – If costs are paid by the landlord and not reimbursed by the tenant, they will be deductible. Costs charged to tenants are deductible if amounts collected are included in rental income.

Multiple Owners: When two or more taxpayers jointly own a revenue property, it is necessary to determine whether they own the property as co-owners or as partners in a partnership. All members of a partnership must make the same CCA claim which is then allocated to each partner individually. Co-owners may each make different CCA claims in respect of the same rental property. . .that is they can choose to claim some or none of their available CCA deduction.

Chapter 4 will cover the consequences of revenue property dispositions.

Avoid Attribution Rules on family income splitting

Canadians are taxed as individuals, not as economic units or households. And, because of the advantages under our progressive tax system with its graduated tax rates—that is, the more you earn the higher your rate of tax—we are generally prohibited from obtaining a tax advantage by splitting income with family members.

These are called the Attribution Rules. Specifically, the Income Tax Act covers these rules as follows:

Transfers and loans to spouse or common-law partner. If an individual transfers or loans property either directly or indirectly, by means of a trust or any other means to the spouse or common-law partner for that person's benefit, any resulting income or loss from that property is taxable to the transferor.

> **Essential TAX FACT #94**
>
> If a taxpayer gifts or transfers money or assets to his or her spouse or minor children, the result is this: income is usually "attributed back" to the taxpayer (transferor) and added to his or her income.

Transfers and loans to minors. Where property is transferred or loaned either directly or indirectly to a person who is under 18 and who does not deal with the transferor at arm's length or who is the niece or nephew of the transferor, the income or loss resulting from such property is reported by the transferor until the transferee attains 18 years of age.

Capital Gain orLoss. When property that is transferred to the individual's spouse or common-law partner earns taxable capital gains (or losses), such income or loss will be reported by the transferor. When property that is transferred to a minor, the resulting capital gain or loss is deemed to be the income of the minor.

These rules thwart an otherwise perfect investment opportunity: the transfer of assets from the higher earner to the lower earners in the family to take advantage of their lower tax brackets, when reporting resulting income, leading to lower total tax payable, and more after-tax funds for the family!

However, where there are rules, there are exceptions, which is true of the Attribution Rules as well. But, let's cover off the tax filing basics on income splitting first:

Facts on Asset Transfers to the Spouse

- Assets transferred to a spouse will result in the income and capital gains resulting from investment of those funds to be taxed in the transferor's hands.

- Where a spouse guarantees the repayment of a loan, made for investment purposes to the other spouse, attribution will apply to any income earned from the loaned funds.

Facts on Asset Transfers to a Minor Child

- Income resulting from assets transferred to a minor child will trigger attribution of dividend and interest income, but not capital gains

There are certain exceptions to the Attribution Rules:

- *Spousal RRSPs.* Investments made in a spouse's name, as a contribution to a spousal RRSP will not be subject to attribution.

- *Wages paid to spouse and children.* Where a spouse or children receive a wage from the family business, attribution rules won't apply if the wage is reasonable, and is included in the recipient's income.

- *Interest income from Child Tax Benefit (CTB) payments.* If these amounts are invested in the name of a child, the interest income will not be subject to attribution. In other words, interest, dividends and capital gains may be reported in the hands of the child. Be sure this account remains untainted by birthday money and other gifts.

- *Joint Accounts.* T5 Slips are issued by banks in the names of the account holders to report earnings on investments including interest, dividends and other sources. This, however, does not mean that the income on those slips is taxable to those whose names are on the slips. Instead, report income on the return of the individuals who contributed the funds to the account in the proportion that the funds were supplied.

For example, if only one spouse in a family works and is the source of all of the deposits, then all of the interest earned on the account is taxable to that person, no matter whose name is on the account.

• *Transfers for fair market consideration:* The Attribution Rules will not apply to any income, gain or loss from transferred property if, at the time of transfer, consideration was paid for the equivalent of fair market value for the transferred property by the transferee.

• *Transfers for indebtedness:* The Attribution Rules on investment income will not apply if the lower earning spouse borrowed capital from higher earner, and the parties signed a bona fide loan that bore an interest rate equal to the *lesser* of:
  – the "prescribed" interest rates in effect at the time the indebtedness was incurred and
  – the rate that would have been charged by a commercial lender.

• *Payment of Interest on Inter-Spousal Loans:* Interest must actually be paid on the indebtedness incurred by the spouse, under a formal loan agreement described above at the prescribed interest rate by January 30 of each year, following the tax year, or the loan will be subject to attribution.

• *Transfers at Fair Market Value.* When property is transferred to the spouse for fair market value, that is, the spouse actually pays for the property at market rates a non-related person would pay, income from the asset after the transfer is taxed to the new owner.

• *Assets transferred to an adult child (over 18)* will in general not be subject to attribution. However, when income splitting is the main reason for the loan to an adult child, the income will be attributed back to the transferor. An exception again occurs when a bona fide loan is drawn up with interest payable as described above, by January 30 of the year following the end of the calendar year.

- *When Spouses Live Apart.* If spouses are living separate and apart due to relationship breakdown, they can jointly elect to have Attribution Rules not apply to the period in which they were living apart. Attribution Rules do not apply after a divorce is finalized.

- *The Kiddie Tax.* The Attribution Rules will not apply when an amount is included in the calculation of Tax on Split Income on Line 424 on Schedule 1 of the tax return. This special tax was introduced in tax year 2000 on income earned by minor children from their parents' or other relatives' ventures. Specifically, dividends or shareholder benefits earned either directly or through a trust or partnership, from a corporation controlled by someone related to the child, are extracted from the normal tax calculations and reported on *Form T1206* so that tax on this income can be calculated at the highest marginal rates.

- *Assignment of Canada Pension Plan benefits.* It is possible to apply to split CPP benefits equally to each spouse, thereby minimizing tax on that income source in some cases.

- *Investments in Spouse's Business.* Investments in the spouse's or common-law partner's business venture, are not subject to Attribution Rules, as the resulting income is business income as opposed to income from property.

- *Second Generation Earnings.* While the income earned by property transferred to the spouse must be reported by the transferor, any reinvestment of such income, which then earns secondary income, is taxed to the transferee.

- *Spousal Dividend Transfers.* The transfer of dividends from one spouse to another is allowed if by doing so a Spousal Amount is created or increased.

- *Inheritances:* Attribution does not apply to inheritances received by the lower earner.

- *Additional Attribution Avoidance strategies:*
  - Have the higher income spouse pay household and personal expenses, and lower income spouse acquire investments assets with income earned in his or her own right.
  - Reinvest spouse's income tax refunds and refundable tax credits.
  - Contribute to an RESP for your child. Accumulate education savings on a tax-deferred basis, as discussed below.

Maximize tax preferred education savings

An RESP is a tax-assisted savings plan set up for the purposes of funding a beneficiary's future education costs. It also serves as a way to split income earned in the plan off to the beneficiary, who will be taxed at a lower rate than the contributor, as a general rule, when earnings are withdrawn.

A contributor can invest:

- $4,000 per beneficiary per calendar year
- $42,000 per beneficiary as a lifetime maximum.

The following rules apply to RESPs:

- the plan must terminate after 25 years
- minor siblings can substitute as plan beneficiaries if the intended beneficiary does not become a qualifying recipient.

**Essential
TAX FACT #97**

There is a further tax incentive for educational savings under the RESP: the Canada Education Savings Grant.

If the subscriber contributes more than the above limits allow, a penalty tax of 1% per month on the excess amount is imposed. Transfers may be made between RESPs with no income tax consequences.

The subscriber, who contributes money into the plan, does not receive a tax deduction at the time of investment. However, income earned within the plan on the contributions made is tax-deferred until the beneficiary student qualifies to receive education assistance from the plan by starting to attend post-secondary school on a full time basis.

This grant is added to the RESP each year by the Department of Human Resources and Skills Development. The grant is received on a tax-fee basis by the plan. Started in 1998, it provides for a federal grant of 20% of the first $2,000 contributed to an RESP for children under the age of 18.

To receive the money, the beneficiary of the RESP must have a Social Insurance Number. The CESG room of up to $400 a year (20% of $2,000) can be maximized each year including the year the child turns 17. Unused CESG contribution room can be carried forward until the child turns 18, however, the grant may not exceed $800 a year. This means that the catch-up of the grants is limited to two years at a time.

You should also know that the federal budget of March 2004 proposed to increase the grant rate on the first $500 of contributions made to an RESP by low-income families in years before the child turns 17. The proposed rates are as follows:

- For families with qualifying net income of $35,000 or less the rate will be 40% of the first $500 and 20% of the remainder (maximum $100 enhanced grant + $400 normal grant)

- For families with qualifying net income between $35,000 and $70,000 the rate will be 30% of the first $500 and 20% of the remainder (maximum $50 enhanced grant + $400 normal grant)

These income thresholds will be indexed to inflation in future years.

The Canada Learning Bond. The March 2004 budget also introduced this new sweetener to the RESP provisions for children born after 2003. The first time a child becomes eligible to receive benefits under the National Child Benefit, which is part of the Child Tax Benefit calculations, an initial Canada Learning Bond entitlement of $500 is available. This will generally happen under one of two circumstances:

Essential TAX FACT #98

A new Canada Learning Bond entitlement will be earned by certain low income earners to maximize RESP savings opportunities.

- The year of birth or

- a subsequent year if the family net income is too high in the year of birth.

The entitlement is $100 in each subsequent year that the family qualifies for the NCB until the year the child turns 15. Once 16, the CLB is no longer allocated to the child.

In order to turn the entitlement into real money, the Canada Learning Bond must be transferred into a Registered Education Saving Plan (RESP) for the benefit of the child. This can be done at any time before the child turns 21. If the CLB is not transferred to an RESP by the time the child turns 21, the entitlement will be lost.

The Canada Learning Bond transfers will not otherwise affect the limits of contributions to the RESP. CLB amounts will not be eligible for the Canada Education Savings Grant.

Also, no interest will be paid on unclaimed Canada Learning Bonds so it will be important that the CLB be transferred to an RESP as quickly as possible so that the amount can begin to earn income.

In the year the baby is born, if the parents are eligible for the National Child Benefit Supplement, the parents should:

- Obtain a social insurance number for the child (required for an RESP)
- Open an RESP account with the new child as beneficiary
- Apply to have the Canada Learning Bond amount transferred to the new RESP.

Education Assistance Payments. When a student is ready to go to post-secondary school full time, payments can be made out of an RESP. These are called Education Assistance Payments (EAPs). The amounts represent earnings in the plan and are taxable to the student on Line 130 of the return. Contributions may be returned to the subscriber or paid to the student with no income tax consequences.

The maximum EAP is $5,000 until the student has completed 13 consecutive weeks in a qualifying education program at a post-secondary educational institution. Once the 13-weeks have been completed, there is no limit to the amount that may be withdrawn from the plan. However, if, for a period of 12 months, the student does not enroll in a qualifying education program, the 13-week period and the $5,000 limitation will be imposed again.

If the student does not attend post-secondary school by the time s/he reaches the age of 21, and there are no qualifying substitute beneficiaries, the contributions can go back to the original subscriber.

However, the income earned in the plan over the years will become taxable to the subscriber, and the income is subject to a special penalty tax of 20% in addition to the regular taxes payable. Such income inclusions are called "Accumulated Income Payments" or AIPs. *Form T1172* must be completed to compute this tax.

As an alternative, if the subscriber has unused RRSP contribution room, AIPs can be transferred into the subscriber's RRSP, up to a lifetime maximum of $50,000. If amounts are transferred to an RRSP, *Form T1171* may be used to reduce or eliminate tax withheld on the AIP.

Note, the CESG will form part of the EAPs. If amounts are withdrawn from the RESP for purposes other than EAP payments, the lesser of the undistributed CESG amounts and 20% of the amount withdrawn will be returned to the Department of Human Resources by the RESP. Should the beneficiary be required to repay any CESG amounts paid to him as Educational Assistance Payments, a deduction for the amount repaid may be taken.

Deduct professional fees, interest & carrying charges

When you incur expenses to invest your money, a tax deduction is possible but only if the expenses are incurred to earn income outside of registered accounts. Known as "carrying charges," eligible expenses are all reported on *Schedule 4 – Statement of Investment Income*. The total carrying charges are then deducted on Line 221 and serve to offset other income of the year, so they can be lucrative. Examples of deductible carrying charges include:

- The safety deposit box
- Accounting fees relating to the preparation of tax schedules for investment reporting (See Accounting and Legal Fees)
- Investment counsel fees. This does not include commissions paid on buying or selling investments. These commissions form part of the Adjusted Cost Base of the investment, or reduce proceeds of disposition from the investment.
- Taxable benefit reported on the T4 Slip for employer-provided loans that were used for investment purposes
- Canada Savings Bonds payroll deduction charge
- Life insurance policy interest costs if an investment loan was taken against cash values
- Management or safe custody fees
- Foreign non-business taxes not claimed as a federal or provincial foreign Tax Credit
- Interest paid on investment loans if there is a reasonable expectation of income from the investment, even if the value of the investment has diminished.
- Brokerage fees* paid to secure debt obligations such as strip bonds, may be claimed as a deduction. In addition, broker fees paid for investment counsel are deductible as a carrying charge. To be deductible, these

investment counsel fees must be specific to buying and selling specific securities or to manage those securities. If they are charged to the client by a stockbroker who also may be charging a commission for the trades themselves, the investment counsel fees must be separately billed.

*Note that if broker fees are paid to buy the shares or other securities, they are treated as part of the Adjusted Cost Base (ACB) of the securities and reported on *Schedule 3 Capital Gains and Losses* instead. When broker fees are paid to sell securities, they are deducted from the proceeds received. In other words, brokerage fees to sell securities reduce the net proceeds. This will either decrease a capital gain realized, or increase a capital loss.

Minimize quarterly instalment payment requirements

Taxpayers who, upon completion of their annual tax returns, have a net tax owing of more than $2,000 (before taking into account any instalment payments made) in the current tax year and either:

- the previous tax year or
- the second previous tax year

are required to pay their taxes by making instalment payments. For residents of Quebec, the threshold is $1,200.

Farmers and fishermen are permitted to make one instalment of at least two-thirds of the estimated taxes for the year. This payment is due by December 31 of the taxation year. All others are required to remit the estimated taxes in quarterly instalments. Due dates are:

- March 15
- June 15
- September 15
- December 15

Essential TAX FACT #99

It pays to monitor your quarterly instalment payment. Better to invest in yourself all year long, than to overpay the government.

If the CRA sends you an instalment notice, based on tax results of your previous filings, there will be no penalties or instalment interest charged so long as you pay the amounts specified by the dates specified on the notice, regardless of whether the amount properly reflects the taxes due for the year. This is called the "no calc" or "no calculation" method.

Most people don't know there are two other ways to estimate instalment payments: the "current year" and the "prior year" method, which could serve to decrease instalments, thereby freeing up new capital for investment purposes.

- *Current-Year Option* – under this option, the taxpayer's income tax liability for the current taxation year is estimated and, if the estimate exceeds $2,000 then one-quarter of the estimated amount is due on each of the four due dates. Interest will be charged under this method when taxes prepaid are insufficient and late.

- *Prior-Year Option* – under this option, total instalments for the year are equal to the net taxes due from the prior year. If the amounts are paid on time throughout the year but insufficient when the return is filed, no addition interest will be charged.

The interest rate charged by CRA is prescribed quarterly and interest is compounded daily. If one or more instalment payment is late, the interest payable may be offset by making a subsequent payment early. This "contra" interest on the early instalment payment will be used to offset the interest on the late instalment. However, it doesn't work the other way: if CRA has overcollected instalments, no interest is paid out to you.

**Essential
TAX FACT #100**

Instalment tax payments are no longer payable on or after the day a taxpayer dies.

Penalties for Delinquent Instalments. When the interest charge payable to CRA is more than $1,000, a penalty is assessed. This penalty is 50% of the interest payable minus the greater of $1,000 and 25% of the instalment interest, calculated as if no instalments had been made for the year. At current rates, instalments of more than $12,000 are needed to reach the threshold for this penalty.

CHAPTER SUMMATION:
ESSENTIAL TAX FILING FACTS FOR INVESTORS

1. The more after-tax dollars you have to invest today, the wealthier you'll be in the future.

2. Your net income can be reduced contributions to registered accounts such as the RPP and RRSP.

3. When your investment earnings compound on a tax-deferred basis within a registered account, you tap into the most tax efficient way to earn investment income.

4. The tax deduction for your RRSP contribution need not be taken in full in the year you make it—you can choose to save or defer the deduction into the future.

5. Income from a property specifically does not include capital gains or losses from the disposition of such property.

6. Canada's "self assessment" system puts the onus of proof on you the taxpayer to prove gross and net income earned.

7. The marginal tax rate is the rate of tax paid on the next dollar earned or the next dollar spent. Income source, income level and rates of taxes applied are needed to calculate this.

8. Income earned on money or assets transferred to the taxpayer's spouse or minor children will usually be "attributed back" to the transferor.

9. The Attribution Rules will apply to joint accounts held by parents and minor children as well as spouses.

10. Attribution Rules can be avoided in education savings by investing in an RESP.

11. Many Canadians buy CSBs on a payroll deduction plan, in which case the interest charge paid is deductible on Line 221 as a carrying charge.

12. Accrued interest earned inside a non-registered account is reported annually on the anniversary date of the investment contract.

13. In general when interest rates rise, the value of a bond or debenture paying a fixed rate of interest will decrease, and vice versa.

14. A taxpayer can earn over $30,000 in dividends on a tax free basis, depending on the province of residence. But because the dividend "gross up" artificially increases net income, it may reduce refundable or non-refundable tax credits.

15. Income earned on mutual funds will increase cost base if reinvested, which can affect your eventual gain or loss when you sell them.

16. Within a segregated fund, the policyholder does not own the units; the segregated fund trust does. Therefore income allocations do not affect the value of the fund.

17. Real estate investors can earn investment income, too.

18. It pays to monitor your quarterly instalment payment. Better to invest in yourself all year long, than to overpay the government.

NOW PUT MORE MONEY IN YOUR POCKET ALL YEAR LONG...

PERSPECTIVE

- To accumulate capital, start a disciplined savings plan today.

- Build equity by first investing in a tax exempt principal residence.

- Reduce non-deductible debt. Try to eliminate interest paid on credit card balances and minimize interest costs on principle residences. Then use your new found cash to invest wisely.

- Split income with family members. Know that better tax results can be achieved for the family unit as a whole when income is distributed amongst the family members. So plan to split income with family members whenever possible, but avoid Attribution Rules.

- Understand the effects of time and rates of return: $1000 invested now and then again at the start of each year, with a semi-annual compounding frequency will grow to just over $5500 in 5 years at 4% interest. At 10% that same investment would grow to close to $6300—14% more. But if you hold on to that investment pattern for 25 years, your investment of $1000 a year will grow to over $42,000 at 4% and over $103,000 at 10%.

- The "Rule of 72" tells us that it will take 18 years for your investment to double at a 4% rate of return—but only 7.2 years at 10%. So rate is very important, especially when the reality of inflation erosion is factored into your investments' performance.

- Earn a bonus with an RRSP. Tax sheltering can help you hedge inflation erosion and give a lift to your rates of return. One of the best ways to do so is through the use of an RRSP. The accumulation results are dramatic. So make that your first priority.

- Be more tax efficient within your non-registered accounts by diversifying your income sources.

ESSENTIAL TAX FACTS FOR WEALTH PRESERVATION

The Future is Now. . .if you are a dedicated investor, you will know how difficult it is to save in the first place, not to mention keep ahead of market risk, taxes and inflation. How do you now cash out in a tax efficient manner to fund lifecycle change?

- How much more do you need?
- Choose with tax order and preserve capital
- Embrace tax consequences of family asset transfers first
- Timing and history is key in understanding capital gains tax
- Manage the disposition of your tax prepaid assets
- Maximize lucrative tax exemptions for personal residences
- Optimize tax rules on other real estate holdings
- Claim capital losses properly to preserve wealth
- Report disposition of shareholdings with acumen
- Take a "no surprises" approach to interest deductibility and debt forgiveness
- Implement tax preferred separations and final departures
- Leverage your RRSP with tax free withdrawals
- Create a tax efficient pension with your RRSP assets

How much more do you need?

One of the reasons why today's Canadians are wealthier than generations before is that their financial assets include real estate and private pension accumulations. Increasingly, savings in registered and unregistered accounts are enhancing Canadians' net worth, which averages about $250,000 across the country.

**Essential
TAX FACT #101**

Canadians could be so much wealthier, if they took full advantage of the most common and lucrative tax preference: the RRSP.

It is estimated that 90% of Canadians don't top up their available RRSP contribution room. This is a surprising lack of commitment to tax savings today—tax deferred wealth accumulation for tomorrow.

Further, according to CRA statistics available at the time of writing, only 17% or 3.6 Million tax filers contributed to a Registered Pension Plan ($7.5 Million) through their employer, while 24% or 5.6 Million taxfilers contributed $25 Million in deductible RRSP contributions. Average household pension accumulations are approximately $120,000 with about $56,000 of those in RRSPs.

This won't go far for the "Freedom 55" crowd who live to be 85—only $4000 annually at the top end, will barely fund a vacation, especially after deducting tax.

It's important, in that context, to gaze into the future, to the time when your capital accumulations must support your lifestyle. Ask your financial advisors for help in projecting your income needs. Integrate this with a tax-efficient savings withdrawal plan, especially during periods of change. Your capital will go farther if you take the time to study your tax options before accessing funds within your registered or unregistered accounts or leveraging your investments in real estate.

You may wish to ask some very specific questions: What are your options for preserving assets when you want to transfer them to family members during your lifetime? How are your assets going to be taxed upon death or divorce? or Should certain assets be disposed of sooner than others? Are there special rules for transfers of assets within the family? Finally, how can you maximize your RRSP withdrawals when it is time to start a retirement annuity?

By planning with a tax focus, your lifetime achievements in accumulating capital will not only support you as you transition into to new life cycles, but you will have an excellent chance of preserving capital which continues to grow while you tap in

Choose a tax order to preserve capital

Consider your needs carefully before you initiate a taxable disposition of your savings. Are you cashing in to fund a short term financial dilemma, due to marital change or to fund retirement lifestyles? Your reasons for tapping into your capital accumulations will drive the choice of investment and order of disposition. To preserve your wealth in times of change, think about following a tax efficient order of disposition to "realize" the least amount of taxable income possible.

You may also wish to think of your capital accumulations within three broad categories as you contemplate your options:

1. *Tax exempt assets:* This can include your principal residence and proceeds you will receive from life insurance policies. It may be possible to tap into the equity built up in these assets first, as proceeds will usually be tax exempt. It may also be possible to leverage equity in these assets, in some cases.

2. *Tax pre-paid assets:* This includes investments held inside non-registered accounts, like personal property, shares, mutual funds and bonds, and revenue properties. These investments will have been made on a tax pre-paid basis—that is, no tax deduction is allowed when the principal is invested. Depending on asset class, your marginal tax bracket and market timing, it is best to realize profits from these sources on a planned basis, especially in times of change.

3. *Tax-assisted accumulations:* This commonly includes accumulations within registered accounts, such as an RRSP, upon which a tax deduction was received when capital was invested. The purpose of this capital is to fund specific lifecycle needs—your retirement, for example—

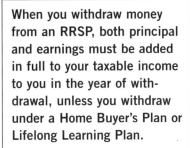

Essential TAX FACT #102

When you withdraw money from an RRSP, both principal and earnings must be added in full to your taxable income to you in the year of withdrawal, unless you withdraw under a Home Buyer's Plan or Lifelong Learning Plan.

Essential
TAX FACT #103

You can often use the tax system to create new capital without coming up with any new money, by "flipping" assets held in a non-registered account into an RRSP, thereby creating new tax savings.

Essential
TAX FACT #104

The increase in value in capital assets held outside registered accounts will accrue on a tax deferred basis until they are disposed of. Then only 50% of the gain will be taxable. Losses incurred on most capital assets, however, are only deductible against capital gains, but may qualify for carryover provisions.

when other actively earned income sources diminish or disappear. Because earnings are sheltered within the plan along the way, it is often, but not always, best to continue the tax deferral as long as possible, to preserve the tax preferences. Tax efficient withdrawal strategies should take into account marginal tax rates during a taxpayer's lifetime and at death, because unlike other asset dispositions, the withdrawal of capital from an RRSP results in fully taxable income.

Especially when under pressure, many people think about withdrawing money from their RRSPs first. This may or may not be the best place to start.

If you are trying to fund the purchase of a new home or returning to post-secondary school, it could be a good idea, as you can tap into the RRSP on a tax free basis under the Home Buyer's Plan or Lifelong Learning Plans. We'll discuss this in more detail later.

If the lump sum you need is smaller and based on a short term need, (you owe CRA an unexpected balance due, your credit cards are maxed, or you have to pay for a funeral) you may wish to contribute to rather than withdraw from an RRSP, thereby creating new capital with tax savings. This can work if you are age eligible and have the contribution room and may not require any new capital, as you may be able to flip assets held outside registered accounts into an RRSP to create the deduction.

If, on the other hand, the sums you need are large, or if lifecycle changes require asset dispositions due to illness, death, divorce or moves to another city to take a job, you will want to know special rules on how and when to report capital gains and preserve losses due to other asset dispositions.

You may be able to control when you generate the sale or asset transfer (over two tax years for example) or choose investments that allow you to blend the withdrawal of tax-prepaid principal and taxable earnings—all with the goal of minimizing your over-all tax cost.

But, of course, tapping into those significant resources will only work if you are ready to sell, or if in fact, your asset is accessible to you within your required time lines.

In short, depending on the diversity of your portfolio, your marginal tax bracket, and your family tax filing profile, there are several options for income and equity creation to discuss with your financial advisors.

**Essential
TAX FACT #105**

You might even own some tax exempt assets. . .for most people that includes one principal residence per household. Others own shares of a qualifying small business corporation, which may qualify for a Capital Gains Exemption of up to $500,000. The benefits received from life insurance policies are also tax exempt to the beneficiary

Embrace tax consequences of family asset transfers first

To everything there is a season. . .perhaps it is time to move your ailing parents into your home to better take care of them. Should you sell their home? Perhaps your parents have decided it is time to pass the cottage to you and your siblings. At what value will you inherit this now? Perhaps you have decided to leave the country to take a job overseas. . .how can you avoid departure taxes if you don't wish to sell your assets?

Many of these real life scenarios result in taxable consequences without the exchange of money. So to begin any discussion on wealth

**Essential
TAX FACT #106**

Sometimes, assets are sold to strangers or transferred to relatives. In fact, assets can often be transferred without immediate tax consequences to spouses or children. This is called a "tax free rollover" to a non-arm's length party.

preservation in times of change, you will need to understand your obligations and opportunities when assets are transferred to family members. To do so, you need to understand some tax jargon:

• "Arm's length" transactions are those undertaken with an unrelated person.

• "Non-arm's length" persons are related to the taxpayer by blood, marriage or adoption, or those affiliated with the taxpayer, which can include a common-law partner, corporation, partnership or members of a group who are affiliated with one another.

For example, when Tom sells his rental property to an unrelated third party, he is conducting business on an arm's length basis. If he sells the property to his wife, Samantha, it is a non-arm's length transaction.

The disposal of your assets can be through an actual sale, or upon a "deemed disposition". This might happen upon:

- Death of a taxpayer
- When an asset's use is changed from business to personal
- When property is transferred to a trust or a registered account
- When a taxpayer emigrates
- When an asset is given to another as a gift
- When one asset is exchanged for another
- When an asset is stolen, damaged, destroyed or expropriated
- When shares held are converted, redeemed or cancelled
- When options to acquire or dispose of property expires
- When a debt is settled or cancelled

For example, Marion needed to make an RRSP contribution but she had no cash. Instead, she opted to transfer 100 shares of ABC corporation shares to her self-directed RRSP. Marion will receive an RRSP receipt for the Fair Market Value of the shares and must also report a capital gain—as she is "deemed" to have disposed of the shares at their Fair Market Value.

Essential TAX FACT #107

For most assets transferred by way of gift to a spouse or common law partner, tax consequences of disposition can be deferred until the asset is actually disposed of.

At the time of sale or transfer, the Adjusted Cost Base of your asset (original cost plus or minus certain adjustments) will be subtracted from the proceeds of disposition to properly report the resulting tax consequences. As transfers between family members generally occur without the exchange of money, a deemed disposition occurs. . .but at what value?

At the time of such transfers to a spouse, it is only necessary to report the change of ownership on the transferor's return at the asset's adjusted cost base. This results in a "tax free rollover" of the asset to the spouse.

You can also choose, not to have those general rules apply by making a special request or election when filing the return. In that case, the transfer will be reported at the property's fair market value. The tax consequences will then be addressed immediately on the transferor's return—that is a capital gain or loss could result.

This might be particularly advantageous, for example, if the transferor wants to use up capital loss balances. These are the same basic rules allowed to spouses/common law partners upon death of the taxpayer.

However, when a spouse actually pays Fair Market Value for the asset:

- income earned from the property is reported by the spouse to whom the property is transferred

- later dispositions of the property will be taxed in the transferee spouse's hands

- interest paid on a loan drawn to the transferor will be deductible if the resulting property is used to earn income, and interest is actually paid

- the transferor will report that interest received on his/her tax return.

**Essential
TAX FACT #108**

When assets are transferred to the spouse, resulting income from property and resulting tax consequences on disposition will be attributed back to the transferor unless the receiving spouse actually pays fair market value for the asset or a bona fide loan is drawn up.

**Essential
TAX FACT #109**

When you transfer property to your adult children during your lifetime, the property is always transferred at fair market value and the tax consequences are immediately reported. Timing is important.

Note that the gains or losses from the disposition of capital assets transferred to minor children will be subject to tax on their own returns—often resulting in nil tax. However transfers of assets to adult children are treated differently.

For example, Harold and Edna want to transfer their cottage property to their adult son Jonathan and his wife Jesse this year. At the time of transfer, fair market value will be assessed, and Harold and Edna will use that figure as the "proceeds of disposition" on their tax return. This will normally produce a tax consequence, however, if the property is a principal residence, a special tax exemption may be tapped.

Taxable and tax-free rollovers are also calculated upon personal departure—emigration, separation or divorce or death of the taxpayer. Speak to your tax and financial advisors before these changes occur, wherever possible and understand the tax calculations behind any resulting capital gain and loss applications.

Timing and history is key in understanding capital gains tax

In the last chapter, we focused on capital accumulation and tax efficient income investing along the way. There you learned that the value of a capital asset accrues on a tax deferred basis until disposition—actual or deemed—even when held outside a registered account. For the purpose of the discussion below, we will be focusing on dispositions of those assets held outside of registered accounts.

Essential TAX FACT #110

There are two unique characteristics of capital assets. The first is that capital gains or losses only arise when an asset is actually disposed of. This leads to the second characteristic: any increase in the value of a qualifying asset while it is held is not taxable until it is disposed of.

When an income-producing asset, is disposed of for an amount greater than what it was originally purchased for, a capital gain will arise. If an asset is disposed of for less than its original cost, a capital loss is the result.

Although it is usually income-producing assets like stocks, bonds and real estate that fall under the capital gains provisions, certain personal items may also be subject to capital gains tax. Personal assets such as second homes, coins, and rare jewellery are examples.

The amount of a capital gain (or loss) is the difference between the proceeds from disposing of the asset and the adjusted cost base (ACB) of that asset, less any outlays and expenses, as outlined in the last chapter.

To refresh your memory use this equation to compute your capital gains or losses:

$$\text{Proceeds of Disposition} - \text{Adjusted Cost Base} - \text{Outlays and Expenses} = \text{Capital Gain or Loss}$$

The amount of capital gain that is included in income is called the "taxable gain" and this is determined by the capital gains inclusion rate. This has changed a number of times since the introduction of capital gains taxes in 1972, as outlined below:

History of Capital Gains Inclusion Rates

- 1972-1987 and Oct. 18, 2000 to date: 50% (1/2)
- 1988-89 and Feb. 28, 2000 to Oct. 17, 2000   66.67% (2/3)
- 1990-Feb. 27, 2000   75% (3/4)

Because the capital gains inclusion rate changed in 2000, it was possible to have a "blended capital gains inclusion rate" for that year, varying from 50% to 75% depending on when any capital gains or losses were experienced during the year.

Why do you need to know this? Simply stated, to apply your capital losses properly.

When a capital disposition ends in a loss, it must first be applied to reduce all other capital gains income of the year on Schedule 3. If a

Essential
TAX FACT #111

Capital losses may only be used to reduce capital gains in the current year. If losses exceed gains in the current year they may be carried back to reduce capital gains in any of the previous three years or in any subsequent year.

taxable capital gain remains, it is reported as income at Line 127 of the return.

When you bring forward an unused loss from a prior year (incurred in the period 1972 to present) it may be necessary to adjust the loss to today's capital gains inclusion rate—50%.

One more important tax concept to note: Capital loss applications may differ, depending on the classification of asset you own.

Manage disposition of your tax prepaid assets

When you acquire assets outside of a registered account, such as an RRSP, RRIF, or RESP, you must identify the asset classification in order to properly report tax consequences. There are several categories of capital properties on Schedule 3 of the tax return, which is completed in the year you dispose of such assets. These include:

- Personal use properties
- Listed personal properties
- Small business corporation shares
- Identical properties such as mutual funds, publicly traded shares, bonds
- Real estate and other depreciable property

Personal use properties: property owned by the taxpayer primarily for personal use and enjoyment, or the use and enjoyment of their family. This includes such items as a car, boat, cottage, furniture, and other personal effects.

**Essential
TAX FACT #112**

Gains on the disposition of personal-use property are taxable as capital gains, but are subject to "The $1,000 Rule".

That is, both the proceeds and adjusted cost base of the property is recorded as at least $1,000. This rule effectively exempts gains on smaller personal-use items from taxation.

**Essential
TAX FACT #113**

When a part of a personal-use property is disposed of, the $1,000 minimum amount used for the proceeds of disposition and adjusted cost base must be allocated to the entire property and not to each part.

Losses on personal-use property (other than listed personal property) are deemed to be nil because they are considered to be a personal cost of owning the asset. Therefore if the taxpayer owns a cottage for personal use and enjoyment, and then sells that cottage at a loss, there are no tax consequences. Personal residence dispositions are discussed in more detail later.

There is a special rule that prevents the taxpayer from claiming the $1,000 minimum ACB on each piece of a set of properties.

For example, assume a couple wishes to sell a set of silver goblets and cutlery to make enough money for a trip to Cuba. The pieces were acquired for $750 at a garage sale and the couple can now sell each piece for $50. There are 100 pieces in the set. The set is considered to be one property and the $1000 rule will apply only once to the entire sales transaction, even if the pieces are sold to multiple buyers over a period of time.

Listed personal property: This is a special subset of personal-use property which includes rarer pieces such as:

- a print, etch, drawing, painting, sculpture, or other similar work of art,
- jewellery,
- a rare folio, rare manuscript or rare book,
- a stamp, or
- a coin or coin collection.

Essential TAX FACT #114

Losses on listed personal property are allowed, but may only be deducted from gains on other listed personal property.

As with other personal-use property, gains on listed personal property are taxable as capital gains on Schedule 3, but are subject to The $1,000 Rule. However, losses are treated differently for these properties:

Also, where losses on listed personal property exceed gains reported during the year from other listed personal property, unused balances may be carried back and applied against listed personal property gains in any of the prior three years or carried forward to apply against listed personal property gains in any of the following seven years.

Let's now turn our discussion to the disposition of a special type of personal use property, held by the majority of Canadian taxpayers: personal residences which can include a principal residence and one or more vacation properties.

Maximize lucrative tax exemptions for personal residences

Under Canadian tax law, the principal residence is a very important concept. Under current rules, each household (adult taxpayer and/or spouse) can own one principal residence on a tax exempt basis. A principal residence is classified to be "personal-use property", which means that any losses on disposition are deemed to be nil (that's right, not claimable on the tax return).

That's great news! But what is considered to be a principal residence?

This can include a house, cottage, condo, duplex, apartment, or trailer that is ordinarily inhabited by you or some family member at

Essential TAX FACT #115

In most cases, any capital gains on disposition of the principal residence will be exempt from tax.

some time during the year. Except where the principal residence is a share in a co-operative housing corporation, the principal residence also includes the land immediately subjacent to the housing unit and up to one-half hectare of adjacent property that contributes to the use of the housing unit as a residence. If the lot size exceeds one-half hectare, it may be included in the principal residence if it can be shown to be necessary for the use of the housing unit.

Where a family owns *only one property* and lived in the property every year while they owned it, the calculation of the tax exemption on disposition of the property is very straightforward. In these cases there won't be any taxable capital gain on the property.

Essential
TAX FACT #116

When the taxpayer has had only one principal residence, used solely for personal use, no tax reporting is required at the time of disposition, even if a capital gain results.

Essential
TAX FACT #117

Starting in 1982, however, only one property per year can be designated as a principal residence for the family.

Where *more than one property* is owned, and the family uses both residences at some time during the year, the calculation of the principal residence exemption becomes slightly more difficult when one property is disposed.

For periods including 1971 to 1981, each spouse can declare one of the properties as their principal residence. This means that any capital gain that accrued in this period can be sheltered on both properties.

This effectively means that any accrued capital gain on one of the properties (that isn't designated as a principal residence) will be ultimately subject to tax when sold.

The following are important dates to know when assessing the tax consequences of the disposition of family residences:

- *Pre 1972*: no tax will be levied on accrued gains on any capital assets
- *1972 to 1981*: one tax-exempt principal residence allowed in the hands of each spouse
- *1982 to date*: one tax-exempt principal residence allowed to each family unit in which there was legal married status
- *1993 to date*: one tax-exempt principal residence allowed to each conjugal relationship (common-law)

- *1998 to 2001*: same-sex couples could elect conjugal status, thereby limiting their tax exempt residences to one per unit.
- *2001 to date*: same-sex couples required to recognize one tax-exempt principal residence per conjugal relationship.

Essential TAX FACT #118

To calculate the exempt portion of gains on your principal residences, you need a special form: Form T2091 – Designation of a Property as a Principal Residence by an Individual. It's complicated, so get some help from a tax pro to do it right.

In a nutshell, the capital gain on the property is first calculated, using regular rules for capital gains and losses. Once this has been done, the exempt portion is calculated, and then the exempt portion is subtracted from the capital gain. The exempt portion of the gain is calculated as:

$$\text{Total Gain} \quad X \quad \frac{(\text{Number of Years designated as Principal Residence} + 1)}{\text{Number of Years the property was owned}}$$

For example, assume the Smith family sold a cottage last year. They designated it to be their principle residence for the five years in which they owned it. As a result, they paid no taxes on the gain they earned on disposition. This year, however, they are selling their home in the city. This property will be designated the principal residence for 10 of the 15 years they owned it, as the cottage was designated the principal residence in the other 5 years.

Essential TAX FACT #119

The taxable capital gain arrived at on Form T2091, is further reduced by any capital gains election made to use up the $100,000 Capital Gains Deduction on February 22, 1994. This is very important, especially if you are the executor of an estate.

To calculate the exempt portion of the gain on the second property, the capital gain is multiplied by the formula: 10 years of designated ownership plus 1 year divided by 15 years (the number of years the property was owned). Form T2091 would be used to make this calculation and the resulting capital gain would be reported on Schedule 3 of the tax return.

It's most important for anyone who made a capital gains election on capital assets in 1994 to file *Form T664 Capital Gains Election* with their will so that executors can take that 1994 valuation into account on the disposition of assets on the final return.

Mixed Use of Principal Residence. When a taxpayer starts using a principal residence for income-producing (rental, home office) purposes, "change of use" rules must be observed for tax purposes:

- *The Fair Market Value* of the property must be assessed. This is because for tax purposes it is deemed that the property is disposed and then immediately reacquired at the same fair market value, changing its classification from a personal use property to a commercial property. However, under certain circumstances a special election can be made to avoid this (see below).

- *The resulting capital gain,* if any, would be nil if the home was used in each year before this as a principal residence. However, as per the example above, any partial gain would be calculated on Form T2091 if the taxpayer owned and designated a second property to be the principal residence.

- If at some time in the future, the property is converted back to be used as a principal residence only, the same FMV assessment must be done again, as it is considered that there is a deemed disposition and reacquisition of the property for this new use. Tax consequences are then assessed, possibly resulting in a capital gain or a loss. Note that a loss would be allowed because during this period, the property was not personal-use property.

Essential TAX FACT #120

When a principal residence is converted from personal use to income-producing use, an election may be made to ignore the deemed disposition rules normally required under the change of use rules explained above.

Essential TAX FACT #121

Mobile young executives who move with their companies, but wish to established residential roots in a particular place, can still preserve their exempt principal residence status.

The taxpayer can choose, instead, to report the disposition and any capital gain/loss at the time of actual disposition, or at a time they choose to rescind the election.

In fact, the taxpayer can choose to designate the property as his personal residence for up to four years after moving out of the house; longer if it was a requirement of the employer that the taxpayer relocate to a temporary residence that is at least 40 kilometres away. This would be allowed in cases where the taxpayer moves back into the original home upon which the designation is being made, before the end of the calendar year in which employment is terminated.

How do you accomplish all of this?

Simply attach a letter to the tax return in the year of disposition, noting that a S. 45(2) *Election* is being made. Attach a description of the property itself and have the taxpayer sign the election. And be very careful to observe these additional rules:

- Any rental income earned on the property while the taxpayer was absent must be reported in the normal manner.

- Capital Cost Allowance must not be claimed on the property. If it is, you will lose your principal residence exemption on the portion of the property upon which this deduction is claimed .

- No other property can be designated a principal residence at the same time

- The taxpayer must have been a resident or deemed resident of Canada.

Essential TAX FACT #122

It is also possible to make a special election when a taxpayer converts a rental property to a principal residence.

Essential TAX FACT #123

When a principal residence is used in part for business purposes (home office, child care enterprises, etc.), it is possible to retain the principal residence exemption status, provided that no capital cost allowance is claimed on the property.

In that case, there is a deemed disposition at FMV, but the capital gain is reported on actual disposition of the property. This is only allowable, however, if no capital cost allowance was claimed on the property since 1984. Follow the same election procedures as described above, but cite *S. 45(3)*.

Optimize tax rules on other real estate holdings

The disposition of real property can be very lucrative, often depending on its timing, and its use. So, it can pay off handsomely to know the tax rules before you act. The term real estate usually includes buildings and land, but can also include a leasehold interest in real property.

When real estate is held by a taxpayer for personal use and enjoyment, for example, it will generally not earn income, and may be entirely tax exempt if it has always been used as a principal residence, as explained above. In the case of second or subsequent residences that do not produce income, a capital gain or loss would generally be reportable on disposition.

The disposition of commercial real estate, therefore, can produce either:

- a capital gain (or loss) which is 50% taxable under current rules, if property has been used to produce income (generally rents) or

- income from a business, which is fully taxable. This might occur when the property itself is classified as inventory, as in the subdivision and sale of lots.

Essential
TAX FACT #124

Should a personal use property change to an income-producing one, a tax consequence would occur on its change of use (at fair market value), and then again on subsequent disposition.

Real Estate Held as an Income-Producing Investment. When real estate is held to produce rental income, any increase in value is considered to be capital in nature, where capital gains treatment will prevail. However, these calculations upon disposition can be a bit tricky, as the building is considered to be a "depreciable property", while the land is not.

As a depreciable property, buildings used in the course of a taxpayer's rental enterprise or business are eligible for a deduction under the Capital Cost Allowance (CCA) rules. These rules account for the loss of value of an asset over time. Buildings usually generate a deduction of 4% of the asset's undepreciated capital cost (UCC) each year, as they are usually included in CRA's prescribed Class 1. The cost of the building entered in that class will include its component parts, such as heating, light fixtures, air conditioning, sprinkler systems, etc.

When a commercial building is acquired, special reporting rules must be followed:

- Acquisition is considered to have occurred when legal title is acquired, or after the property actually exists, whichever comes first.

- For possessions after 1989, the asset must be "available for use" in order for CCA to be claimed.

- Depreciable assets may sometimes be considered "capital in nature" or as deductible "inventory". When property of the same kind is sold and rented, usually it will be considered to produce income that must be included in income in full.

- No CCA deduction is available on the cost of land; therefore the value of the building must be separated from the total cost to properly schedule the asset for CCA purposes.

- When a building is acquired and then immediately torn down, no CCA deduction will be allowed as the entire cost will be allocated to the value of the land.

- If rental properties are owned by the taxpayer, it is necessary to separately schedule buildings valued at $50,000 or more, rather than to pool the assets together in one class.

- Capital cost allowance deductions are limited to the net income from rental properties, that is, losses cannot be created or increased with these claims.

- In the year the building is acquired, only half the normal CCA claim may be made – regardless of when during the year the building was acquired.

This is because capital gains may occur on the land and/or the building. As well there may be a "recapture" of capital cost allowance deductions claimed on the building. In other cases, a capital loss may occur on the land and a "terminal loss" on the building.

A terminal loss may be claimed if not enough capital cost allowance was taken during the ownership period. When this happens, a deduction can be made against income in full to account for the actual depreciation of the asset. This, of course, is a significant tax advantage in the year the loss occurs. When land and buildings are sold, CRA wants to ensure that allocations made to land and building are not skewed to create such an advantage.

> **Essential**
> **TAX FACT #125**
>
> When a building is disposed of, the proceeds must be allocated to the land and building as well as other depreciable property. Separate calculations may be required to determine the tax consequences of the disposition of each type of property.

Therefore, when the proceeds of disposition allocated to the land exceed its cost, (thereby creating a gain) and the proceeds allocated to the building are less than the Undepreciated Capital Cost (UCC) of the building (thereby creating a fully deductible terminal loss) CRA requires an adjustment. The lesser of:

- The gain on the land and
- The loss on the building

is added to the proceeds from the disposition of the building. The same amount is then subtracted from the proceeds of disposition of the land.

For example, Jim sells a property for $100,000. The property was acquired for $70,000 several years ago. At that time, Jim allocated $60,000 in value to the building and $10,000 to the land. He did not claim a deduction for CCA on the building in the meantime.

Jim decides to allocate $90,000 of the proceeds of disposition to the land (thereby creating an $80,000 capital gain, half of which is taxable), and $10,000 to the building (thereby creating a $50,000 terminal loss, all of which is deductible). The net result would be $10,000 in terminal losses which would offset other income in the year.

CRA would not agree. The loss on the building would be added to its proceeds of disposition, which would result in the elimination of the terminal loss. You will likely want to get some help from a professional in making your allocations upon the sale of your rental properties.

Real Estate Held for Capital Appreciation. When real estate is used in a commercial enterprise, resulting asset dispositions could fall into a grey area. The big question is this: will resulting gains be considered income (100% taxable) rather than capital (50% taxable) in nature?

In deciding on whether a transaction is "income" or "capital" in nature, the courts have considered the following facts on a case-by-case basis:

- the taxpayer's intention with respect to the real estate at the time of its purchase,
- feasibility of the taxpayer's intention,
- geographical location and zoned use of the real estate acquired,
- extent to which intention carried out by the taxpayer,
- evidence that the taxpayer's intention changed after purchase of the real estate,

- the nature of the business, profession, calling or trade of the taxpayer and associates,

- the extent to which borrowed money was used to finance the real estate acquisition and the terms of the financing, if any, arranged,

- the length of time throughout which the real estate was held by the taxpayer,

- the existence of persons other than the taxpayer who share interests in the real estate,

- the nature of the occupation of the other persons who share interest as well as their stated intentions and courses of conduct,

- factors which motivated the sale of the real estate, and

- evidence that the taxpayer and/or associates had dealt extensively in real estate.

In short, is this an income-producing asset (capital property) or inventory to be bought and sold as inventory for profit?

So, based on these factors, if the intention of the taxpayer is to earn income from the sale of real estate, the income is included in income from business. However, if the asset is held for use in the business (i.e. to produce income) the gain on sale is capital in nature.

Vacant land that is capital property used by its owner for the purpose of gaining or producing income will be considered to have been converted to inventory (and therefore subject to business income computation) at the earlier of :

- the time when the owner commences improvements with a view to selling the property, and

Essential TAX FACT #126

The more closely a taxpayer's business or occupation (e.g. a builder, a real estate agent) is related to real estate transactions, the more likely it is that any gain realized by the taxpayer from such a transaction will be considered to be business income rather than a capital gain.

Essential TAX FACT #127

Special rules apply to the disposition of vacant land.

Essential TAX FACT #128

It is CRA's view that the subdivision of farmland or inherited land in order to sell it will not necessarily, constitute a conversion to inventory.

- the time an application is made for approval of subdivision into lots for sale, provided that the taxpayer proceeds with the development of the subdivision.

Mortgage Take Back Arrangements. Sometimes, when a property is sold, the vendor takes back a mortgage. The entire transaction must be reported in the year of disposition, but if the full proceeds of sale are not received, a "reserve" can be created to exclude from income the amount due in the future.

The basic calculation works as follows and will be calculated on Form T2017 before the figures are entered on Schedule 3 of the tax return:

$$\frac{\text{Proceeds not due until after the tax year}}{\text{Total proceeds of disposition}} \quad \text{x} \quad \text{Capital Gain} \quad = \quad \text{Reserve}$$

The capital gains reserve you can claim for amounts not yet received is limited to 5 years for all properties other than family farm property and small business corporation shares.

The maximum percentage of the gain that may be claimed as a reserve is 80% in the first year, 60% in the second, 40% in the third, 20% in the fourth, and in the fifth year, no reserve may be claimed.

For family farm property and small business corporation shares, the maximum reserve is for a period of 10 years. The maximum percentage of the gain that may be claimed as a reserve is 90% in the first year, decreasing by 10% each year so that in the tenth year, no reserve may be taken.

So, what happens when you need to sell or transfer your properties, and the result is a loss in value, rather than a profit? It's important to understand how to claim those losses over a period of years.

Claim capital losses properly to preserve wealth

There may be a silver lining to that dark cloud of asset loss. As you have gleaned from our discussions so far, when a taxpayer incurs certain types of losses on capital property owned outside of registered accounts, they may provide tax advantages. In fact, losses that are not deductible in the year incurred may be carried over to other taxation years in certain cases.

Essential TAX FACT #130

Losses that are applied capital gains of prior years will usually generate a tax refund. That's a very good thing!

Note that the Income Tax Act gives CRA the power to refuse loss recognition, if you don't record them on a timely basis. So, you'll always want to recognize those losses on your tax return in the year they occur. *Form T1A Loss Carryback* is available to help you with the carryover periods.

More good news: CRA will begin paying interest on the outstanding money 30 days after the later of:

- The day on which an application is received
- The day on which an amended return is filed
- The day on which a written request is received
- The first day immediately following the year after the year a loss was incurred.

Essential TAX FACT #131

Net capital losses may be carried back to reduce capital gains reported in any of the previous three taxation years. Amounts that are not applied to prior years may be carried forward indefinitely to apply against capital gains in future years.

With the exception of losses on Listed Personal Property and Personal-Use Property, capital losses incurred in the current year may be applied only against capital gains in the current year. When losses completely offset gains in the current year, any remaining loss becomes a "net capital loss" available for carry over.

Note that when the taxpayer dies, unused capital losses can no longer be carried forward so the unused capital losses (reduced by any capital gains deduction previously claimed by the taxpayer) may be used to reduce other types of income in the year of death or the immediately preceding year.

Net capital losses of other years are deducted on Line 253 of your return.

Note: A special rule applies when investors invest in a limited partnership and lose money.

Limited partnership income is generally reported to the investor on Form T5013 and transferred to the tax return on Line 122 or as rent or other investment income, depending on its source. The partner's at-risk amount is shown on the T5013 slip, together with the partner's income or loss from the partnership. This slip will also note what portion of that loss is a limited partnership loss.

Essential TAX FACT #132

Limited partnership losses not claimed at death or after ten years expire.

Limited partnership losses up to the partner's "at-risk amount" may be deducted against other income. However, when losses exceed Limited Partnership Income, they cannot be used to offset other income or be carried back. Instead, they must be carried forward until the taxpayer reports Limited Partnership Income. In that year, Limited Partnership Losses of Other Years are deducted on Line 251 of the tax return.

Report disposition of shareholdings with acumen

Essential TAX FACT #133

When you trade some of a group of identical shares, you must calculate an average cost each time there is a purchase, in order to properly report a capital gain or loss on Schedule 3.

A taxpayer-investor may hold shares of public or privately held corporations and the tax consequences will differ under each classification.

Public Corporate Holdings. Within the realm of public holdings, it is necessary to determine whether you owned "identical properties". That is, shares or units in a mutual fund that have identical rights and which cannot be distinguished one from the other.

To do so, add the cost base of all shares in the group and divide the sum by the number of shares held.

For example, assume Leila purchased 1000 shares of XYZ company on June 1 and then another 800 shares on August 31. In the first case she paid $10 per share and in the second she paid $12.00 per share. She now owns 1800 shares for an average cost of $10.89 ([1000 x $10 + 800 x $12] / [1000 + 800]).

This is important information in October of the same year, when Leila decides to sell 500 shares to finance her Christmas purchases. At that time she gets $15.00 per share and earns a capital gain of:

$7500 ($15.00 x 500 shares)
− $5445 ($10.89 x 500)
———————————————
= $2055 before brokerage fees

Leila may have wanted to time her winners and losers for maximum tax advantages. That is, offset her capital gains from the transaction above with capital losses generated through "tax loss selling", or timing the sale of capital property which has an unrealized capital loss, so that the loss may be used to offset realized capital gains.

For example, Leila might choose to sell her shares in ABC Company, held outside her RRSP, which she bought for $9 a share and are currently worth $6 per share. That capital loss would offset her gains from XYZ company if the transaction occurred in the same year.

There is no restriction to this type of transaction, except where property identical to the property which is sold at a loss is purchased within 30 days prior to the disposition, or within 30 days after the disposition. Such a "superficial loss" will be disallowed.

Private Corporate Holdings. The Income Tax Act provides for unique tax treatment upon the disposition of privately held shares of a Qualified Small Business Corporation (QSBC). To qualify, the shares must be shares of a small business corporation that was owned by the taxpayer, spouse or common-law partner, or a partnership related to the taxpayer, and:

- The corporation must have actively used at least 90% of its assets (on a fair market value basis) in the operation of the business,

- During the 24 month period prior to the disposition, at least 50% of the corporation's assets (on a fair market value basis) must have been used in an active business carried on primarily in Canada,

- During the 24 month period prior to disposition, the shares must have been shares in a Canadian controlled private corporation (CCPC).

> **Essential TAX FACT #134**
>
> Should a disposition of a qualified small business corporation result in a capital gain, a lifetime capital gains exemption of $500,000 may become available.

The capital gain is reported in the first section of Schedule 3 and the deduction is claimed on *Form T657 Capital Gains Deduction* and Line 254 of the return.

Dispositions that result in losses are also eligible for special tax treatment. If upon disposition or insolvency of shares in a small business corporation, losses arise, 50% of these can be used to offset all other income of the current year, (use line 217 of the tax return). Should excess losses remain, they can be carried forward back to offset other income of the previous three years or carried forward for a period of 10 years (if losses were incurred after 2003). Unapplied losses after this period become capital losses, which can be carried forward and applied against capital gains earned in the future.

These are very lucrative tax provisions that can substantially increase the wealth of corporate small business owners, or ease their resulting loss occurrences if times go bad.

Qualified Farms. For your information, the $500,000 Lifetime Capital Gains Exemption may also be available on qualified farm properties. To be considered a qualified farm property, the enterprise must be one of the following:

- An interest in a family farm partnership owned by the taxpayer or the taxpayer's spouse or common-law partner,
- Shares in a family farm corporation owned by the taxpayer or the taxpayer's spouse or common-law partner,
- Real property (i.e. land, buildings, eligible capital property such as quotas) that was used– in the business of farming by the taxpayer, spouse (or common-law partner), child, or parent in the preceding 24 months prior to disposition. Gross farming income must also exceed income from all other sources for at least two years, or
  – by a family farm corporation or a family farm partnership of the taxpayer, the taxpayer's spouse, common-law partner, child or parent that has farming as a principal business for at least 24 months prior to the disposition.

Take a no-surprises approach to interest deductibility and debt forgiveness

Sometimes, when investors endure difficult times, and can't pay their bills, insolvency or debt forgiveness can result. There are important tax consequences to note when this happens.

Other important tax facts to note on interest deductibility include the following:

- Interest costs on money borrowed to invest in a tax-exempt property or an interest in a life insurance policy are specifically not deductible.

- Interest paid on money borrowed and then used to provide employer and shareholder loans may be deductible, if reasonable, but limited to the income reported from the loans.

- Interest may not be deductible at all if there is no reasonable expectation of profit from the source of the investment.

Essential TAX FACT #135

Interest costs incurred when money is borrowed to make an investment in a capital asset will generally not be deductible as a carrying charge. They are deductible, however, when income from property is earned (interest, dividends, rents or royalties) or where there is potential for such income to be earned.

This is all the result of recent legislation that proposes to limit deductions of interest costs and business losses. Introduced on October 31, 2003 this proposed legislation was slated to come into effect in 2005 at the time of writing.

The legislation also clarifies that "profit" from an investment does not include any capital gains from that investment.

The test for reasonable expectation of cumulative profit will be applied on a yearly basis and if it is determined that it is not reasonable to expect that the taxpayer will have a cumulative profit, the annual losses will not be allowed. However, another test will be applied at the end of the holding period to assess cumulative profit, if the year over year losses pass the reasonable expectation of profit test.

Essential TAX FACT #136

Interest deductibility will hinge upon the direct and current use of the money borrowed and the identification of an income-earning purpose.

In conjunction with this new legislation, CRA released its current interpretations on interest deductibility in an Interpretation Bulletin (IT-533). This should be required reading for all taxpayers who borrow money for business or investment purposes and pay interest costs.

Here are the essential tax facts to know:

- *Tracing/Linking:* The onus is on the taxpayer to trace funds to a current and eligible usage.

- *Chief Source of Income:* The investment loan that gives rise to the interest expense can be for an ancillary, rather than primary income-producing purpose. This will be determined as a question of fact.

- *Borrowing to Acquire Common Shares:* Interest costs on money borrowed to purchase common shares will be deductible if there is a reasonable expectation that dividends will be received at the time the shares were acquired.

- *Money borrowed to redeem shares or return capital.* Interest will be deductible if the capital replaced was previously used for an income-producing purpose.

- *Borrowing to pay dividends.* The interest expense amounts will be deductible.

- *Borrowing to make loans to employees and shareholders.* Interest will be deductible by the employer if there is a reasonable expectation of income from the effort of the employee. Such loans are viewed as a form of remuneration.

- *Borrowing to contribute capital in a company.* Interest may be deductible if the borrowed funds can be linked to an income-producing purpose (e.g. the issuing of dividends).

**Essential
TAX FACT #137**

A deduction for the costs of interest and property taxes paid on undeveloped land is limited to net income from the property. However, should there be little or no income from the land, these expense amounts may be added to the cost base of the land, which will affect the size of future capital gains or losses on disposition.

- *Borrowing for loss utilization.* Interest expenses will be deductible if there is an ancillary purpose of earning income.

- *Leveraged buy-outs.* Interest on money borrowed to acquire common shares will be deductible. CRA comments further by saying there is no arm's length requirement in this case.

Debt Forgiveness. Where a debt is forgiven and a debtor is required to pay an amount less than the actual amount owing, there are a series of tax consequences. The forgiven amount is generally applied to reduce a number of other available tax preferences. Then, any remaining balance of the forgiven debt is added to the taxpayer's income.

In order, the forgiven amount is used to reduce:

- Non-capital loss balances (except for allowable business investment losses)

- Farm losses

- Restricted farm losses

- Net capital losses

- Depreciable property's capital cost and UCC balances

- Cumulative eligible capital

- Resource expenditure balances

- Adjusted cost base of certain capital properties

- Current year capital losses

After these applications are made, unused debt balances are added to income, but a special reserve can be used to minimize tax consequences. When net income is less than $40,000 a year, a deferral of tax is possible. Speak to your tax advisor about these rules.

Essential TAX FACT #138

It is also possible to transfer unused balances of forgiven debt to another taxpayer. But note, where a debt is assumed by another party, the debt is not considered to be forgiven. Therefore, the debt forgiveness rules above do not apply.

Implement tax preferred separations and final departures

Departure from an existing lifestyle, which gives rise to a capital disposition, can happen as a result of a number of personal changes including:

- Separation or divorce
- Death of the taxpayer

In each case there is a deemed disposition of capital assets. However, in the case of marriage breakdown, a tax-free rollover can occur. Here are some essential tax facts:

Separation and Divorce. A couple need not be legally or formally separated for their tax status to change. A couple is considered to be separated if they cease co-habitation for a period of at least 90 days. When a couple separates:

- Each person will be taxed as an individual

- Income and assets will be separated

- Refundable and non-refundable tax credits will be allocated based on individual net income levels

- Spousal RRSP contributions will no longer be allowed

- Income attribution becomes a non-issue. That is, income attribution ends when there is a separation, providing that an election to this effect is made in the year of separation or after separation, and providing that the couple continues to live apart. Therefore the new owner of the property after relationship breakdown is responsible for all subsequent tax consequences on the earnings and capital appreciation (depreciation) of the property.

- RRSP accumulations can be split. Funds that have accumulated in RRSPs may be rolled over on a tax free basis to the ex-spouse when the parties are living apart and if the payments follow a written separation agreement, court order, decree or judgement. The transfer must be made directly between the RRSP plans of the two spouses and one spouse cannot be disqualified because of age (over age 69). The same rules for tax-free transfer of funds apply to RRIF accumulations. *Form T2220* is used to authorize the transfers between the plans.

- Property brought into the marriage by one of the spouses will be considered owned by that person. Generally the property is then assigned to that person during the creation of the separation agreement.

- Transfer of Other Property. Property transferred upon relationship dissolution can be transferred at its adjusted cost base, (or Undepreciated Capital Cost in the case of depreciable property) so that there are no tax consequences at the time of transfer. This applies to property in settlement of marital property rights as well as any other voluntary transfers. That effectively transfers any accrued gains on the property from its original acquisition to the transferee.

Essential TAX FACT #139

By special election, assets may be transferred at their Fair Market Value. This could result in significant tax savings if, for example, the transferor had unused capital losses to apply to the transferred property.

The transferee would also receive a significant tax benefit in that future capital gains would be calculated based on the FMV at the time of transfer. Further, if the FMV of the property is less than its ACB, it may be advantageous to trigger the capital loss. . .this would allow you to offset other capital gains of the year, the previous three years or capital gains realized in the future.

- Also remember to take into account any capital gains election the individuals may have made in February 1994 and apply the elevated adjusted cost base to the deemed disposition brought on by the relationship breakdown.

- New Tax Exempt Principal Residence Status. After separation, CRA recognizes two family units, and therefore it is possible for each to own one tax exempt residence.

Final Departure. Death of a taxpayer generates numerous tax consequences which can be expensive, particularly for single taxpayers (See Chapter 6) In terms of wealth preservation, however, the acquisition of a life insurance policy, can make some sense and can lead to numerous tax advantages, especially if deemed dispositions of capital assets result in a hefty tax bill.

Essential TAX FACT #140

When an individual buys an insurance policy, there is no deduction claimable for the premiums paid. But, subsequent benefits or proceeds paid out to beneficiaries are tax exempt.

For example, if Judy decides to take out a $100,000 insurance policy on herself and name her baby Jane as beneficiary, her premiums will not be deductible. However, when she dies, Jane receives the benefits under the policy, on a tax exempt basis.

Sometimes an investment in an insurance policy can result in taxable income. This will happen on the anniversary day of the policy when accumulating funds within certain policies exceed the policy's adjusted cost basis. The amounts must be reported on an annual accrual basis, but a deduction for any over-accrual can be taken when a taxpayer disposes of an interest in the policy.

Essential
TAX FACT #141

The investment portion of the policy, known as the Cash Surrender Value (CSV) can also be withdrawn by the policy holder. When that happens there may be a capital disposition with tax consequences.

Income earned within whole life or universal life insurance policies will generally accumulate on a tax-exempt basis provided that the policies have a limitation on the size of the investment component. These features should be discussed with your insurance advisor.In addition, the acquisition of a life insurance policy can help to pay the taxes which arise upon the deemed disposition of taxable assets as at the date of death.

It makes sense to prepare early for your terminal wealth—by assessing the place of life insurance in your estate plans.

Leverage Your RRSP with tax free withdrawals

The RRSP is for me, the life insurance is for the kids!

Essential
TAX FACT #142

The RRSP Home Buyers' Plan allows first time home buyers (or those who have not owned a home in the current year or preceding four years) to withdraw up to $20,000 of funds saved within RRSP for the purpose of buying or building a home, on a completely tax-free basis.

This is how many taxpayers think of their retirement and estate planning activities and this can have some merit. In fact, it can make some sense to fund a life insurance policy with the tax savings earned from an RRSP contribution!

Investors generally withdraw money from their RRSPs on a taxable basis to create a monthly pension, or to supplement income in periods of unemployment or maternity leave. The idea is to try to withdraw to supplement your financial requirements with the taxable RRSP withdrawal when other income sources end or are interrupted. It makes less sense to withdraw when marginal tax rates are high. . .unless of course your stellar savings efforts throughout your lifetime have made you a very wealthy person!

It pays to play with a time line and by knowing your marginal tax bracket and rates. As "ordinary income" that is 100% taxable, plan to defer RRSP withdrawals to a new tax year or take money from a lower earner's deposits first, as a way to minimize tax.

But also consider whether you will be in a higher marginal tax bracket at death. . .if so taxable withdrawals during life can be the most tax efficient RRSP withdrawal strategy.

More on creating a tax efficient pension, later. However, here's an important fact: amounts withdrawn from an RRSP are taxable in the year received unless the amount is withdrawn under the Lifelong Learning Plan (LLP) or the Home Buyers' Plan (HBP).

The RRSP can be so much more than a tax assisted retirement savings plan. It can help you buy a new home or invest in yourself by going back to school.

**Essential
TAX FACT #143**

If you contribute to an RRSP in the 90-day period prior to making the HBP withdrawal, and any of the deposit is withdrawn you may not claim an RRSP deduction for the amount of the contribution which was withdrawn.

The withdrawals may be a single amount or the taxpayer may make a series of withdrawals throughout the year as long as the total does not exceed $20,000.

The funds must be repaid back into the RRSP, though over a 15-year period, beginning in the second calendar year after the withdrawal. Amounts which are due and not repaid are included in the taxpayer's income in the year they are due.

It is not necessary that the taxpayer actually use the funds borrowed for the intended purpose, only that they buy or build the qualifying home.

The taxpayer and their spouse or common-law partner may each participate in the plan and together withdraw up to $40,000 ($20,000 each) from their respective RRSPs.

A qualifying home is a housing unit located in Canada. This includes existing homes and those being constructed. Single-family homes, semi-detached homes, townhouses, mobile homes, condominium units, and apartments in duplexes, triplexes, fourplexes, or apartment buildings, all qualify. A share in a co-operative housing corporation that entitles the taxpayer to possess, and gives the taxpayer an equity interest in, a housing unit located in Canada also qualifies.

Other essential tax facts include the following:

- *You must file a return.* Members of the Home Buyers' Plan must file a tax return each year until their HBP balance is zero, regardless of whether they are otherwise required to file.

- *Age ineligibility triggers income.* After the end of the year that the taxpayer turns 69, repayments to the RRSP can no longer be made because the taxpayer may no longer contribute to his RRSP. Thus, in the year the taxpayer turns 69, if there is an outstanding HBP balance, the taxpayer must elect to pay the outstanding balance or include in income each year the required annual repayment.

- *Disabled Persons.* Home Buyers' Plan withdrawals can also be used for the purpose of making home renovations or purchasing a compatible home to meet the needs of a disabled person. For HBP purposes, a disabled person is an individual who qualifies for the disability amount or a person related by blood, marriage, or adoption to a person who is eligible to claim the disability amount for the year of the HBP withdrawal. Disabled persons need not be first-time homebuyers to participate in the HBP.

- *Effect of Emigration.* If a HBP participant becomes a non-resident, the outstanding balance must be repaid before the return for the year of emigration is filed but no later than 60 days after becoming a non-resident.

- *Year of Death.* In the year of death, the full outstanding amount under the Home Buyers' Plan must be repaid (or included in income of the taxpayer) unless, at the time of death, the taxpayer had a spouse or common-law partner and that individual elects jointly with the deceased's legal representative to make the payments under the Home Buyers' Plan. This election may be made in the form of a letter attached to the deceased taxpayer's final return.

The funds must be paid back into the RRSP, over a 10-year period, beginning in the fifth calendar year after the withdrawal or the year after the student ceases to be a full-time student for at least three months in the year, whichever comes first. Amounts which are due and not repaid are included in the taxpayer's income in the year they are due.

Here are some additional tax facts:

- *MultipleWithdrawals.* Taxpayers are free to participate in the LLP plan again once they have repaid the amount borrowed.

- *Use of Funds.* It is not necessary that the taxpayer actually use the funds borrowed for the intended purpose, only that they become a full-time student.

- *Use by the Disabled.* For LLP purposes, a disabled person is an individual who qualifies for the disability amount for the year of the LLP withdrawal. Disabled persons need not be full-time students to qualify.

- *Emigration.* If a LLP participant becomes a non-resident, the outstanding balance must be repaid before the return for the year of emigration is filed but no later than 60 days after becoming a non-resident.

- *Death.* In the year of death, the full outstanding amount under the Lifelong Learning Plan must be repaid (or included in income of the taxpayer) unless, at the time of death, the taxpayer had a spouse or common-law partner. That survivor could then elect jointly with the deceased's legal representative to resume making the payments on a tax exempt basis.

- *Qualifying Programs.* A qualifying educational program is an educational program that:
  – lasts three consecutive months or more; and
  – requires a student to spend 10 hours or more per week on courses or work in the program. Courses or work includes lectures, practical training, and laboratory work, as well as research time spent on a post-graduate thesis. It does not include study time.

Create a Tax Efficient Pension with your RRSP

Well, imagine: you have spent much of your life accumulating money within your RRSP and now it is time to spend it! When the taxpayer becomes age-ineligible (the year in which age 70 is reached), runs out of contribution room, or when it is simply time to start a pension benefit, there are several options to choose from for creating income:

The RRSP accumulations can be taken out in a lump sum (not usually a good idea as the amounts will be taxed at the highest marginal rate at that time).

Withdrawals from an RRSP will be reported on the taxpayer's T4RSP slip, recorded as income on Line 115 if they represent a periodic pension withdrawal or otherwise, Line 129. Withdrawals will be subject to withholding tax at the following rates:

Up to $5,000	10%
$5,000 to $15,000	20%
Above $15,000	30%

Especially when you make a lump sum withdrawal from your RRSP, it is important for you to take this withholding tax into consideration before you make a withdrawal, to ensure you end up with the exact amount of funds you need for the purpose you have in mind.

Withdrawals of Undeducted Amounts and Overcontributions. Sometimes you'll want to withdraw money from an RRSP because you have undeducted contributions, or over-contributions. Such withdrawals are not taxable.

RRSP over-contributions. Sometimes taxpayers will contribute more than their allowable RRSP room. This can happen when you instruct your employer to make RRSP contributions on your behalf through a payroll deduction plan, but forget to tell him about a change in your contribution room due to a tax reassessment.

Essential TAX FACT #145

Stay away from making "excess contributions". These are RRSP contributions which exceed your contribution room plus $2000.

To cushion errors in contributions due to fluctuating RRSP room, an overcontribution limit of $2000 is allowed without penalty. Many taxpayers, in fact, use that rule for tax planning purposes: it's a great way to make even more tax deferred income within your RRSP.

Debbie for example, has RRSP contribution room of $5000, which she has contributed. But she is allowed to contribute $2000 more without penalty, and decides to do so to earn tax deferred investment income while the money is in the plan.

Also note the following in managing your RRSP withdrawals:

- *Withdrawal of undeducted contributions.* Amounts contributed to the taxpayer's RRSP and not yet deducted may be withdrawn tax-free and with no withholding taxes by filing Form T3012A, Tax Deduction Waiver on the Refund of Your Undeducted RRSP Contributions. The amount withdrawn will be included on a T4RSP slip and must be reported as income. The taxpayer may, however, claim an offsetting deduction on the tax return. Taxpayers who withdraw undeducted contributions without using *Form T3012A* will have tax withheld but may use *Form T746* to calculate their allowable deduction on line 232.

- *Contributions in Excess of Overcontribution Limits.* Excess RRSP contributions are subject to a penalty tax of 1% per month on the excess. A complicated form called a T1-OVP must be completed in that case and the penalty must be paid by March 31 of the year following the cumulative excesses. Penalties will accrue until the excess contributions are withdrawn from the RRSP. You'll want to ask a professional to help you with this form.

- *Special Rule for Minors.* Taxpayers who are over the age of 18 may contribute the full amount of their contribution room plus a $2,000 overcontribution. This is not possible for taxpayers who are minors.

Tax Free Transfers to an RRSP. The following capital sources may be transferred to the taxpayer's RRSP on a tax free basis over and above the normal RRSP contribution limits plus the $2000 allowable overcontribution:

- *Eligible Retiring Allowances.* Amounts received on job termination as a severance package may be rolled over into an RRSP on a tax free basis depending on certain conditions. *For service after 1995*, no RRSP rollover is allowed. *For service after 1988 and before 1996*, a single limit of $2000 per year of service can be rolled into an RRSP. And *for service before 1989*, it is possible to roll over $2000 for each year of service plus another $1500 for each year in which the employer's contributions to the company pension plan did not vest in the employee. The eligible amount will be shown on the T4A from the former employer.

- *Funds from another RRSP.* A taxpayer may request a direct transfer of RRSP accumulations from one RRSP to another RRSP under which he is that annuitant. Form T2033 may be used to effect the transfer.

- *Funds from a Spouse's RRSP.* Upon the breakdown of a marriage or common-law relationship, where the terms of a separation or divorce agreement require that the funds from one spouse's RRSP be transferred to the other, the funds may be transferred tax free. Form T2220 must be used.

- *RPP amounts.* When a taxpayer ceases to belong to an RPP, the funds from the RPP be transferred to his RRSP. Form T2151 must be used.

- *DPSP accumulations.* A taxpayer may transfer funds from his DPSP to his RRSP. Form T2151 must be used.

- *Foreign pension receipts.* Lump sum amounts received from a foreign pension plan in respect of a period while the taxpayer was a non-resident may be transferred to the taxpayer's RRSP. Amounts that are exempt from tax under a tax treaty with the foreign country may not be transferred.

- *Saskatchewan Pension Plan amounts.* A lump sum payment out of the Saskatchewan pension plan may be transferred to the taxpayer's RRSP tax free.

Tax Free Transfers from an RRSP. The following funds from a taxpayer's RRSP may be transferred on a tax free basis to:

- *Registered Pension Plan* (only possible if the RPP terms allow this). *Form T2033* may be used.

- *Another RRSP*

- *The RRSP of a spouse or former spouse on breakdown of marriage or common-law relationship*

- *A RRIF.* A taxpayer may transfer funds from his RRSP to a RRIF under which he is the annuitant. Form T2033 must be used.

- *The RRIF of a spouse or former spouse on breakdown of marriage or common-law relationship.* Form T2220 must be used.

- *An annuity* – Amounts can be transferred from the taxpayer's RRSP to an annuity contract for the life of the taxpayer or jointly of the taxpayer and the taxpayer's spouse or common-law partner with or without a guarantee period. If there is a guarantee period, it may not be for a period longer than until the taxpayer (or spouse or common-law partner) reaches 90 years old.

- *RRSP of spouse or former spouse or dependant on death.*

Creating your Pension. When it comes time to create your periodic pension withdrawals from an RRSP, the accumulations will generally be transferred into one of two investment vehicles that will enable a periodic taxable income:

- *an annuity* (which provides for equal monthly payments over a period of time)

- *a Registered Retirement Income Funds (RRIF)*, which provides for gradually increasing payments over time.

Under a RRIF, a minimum amount must be withdrawn according to a predetermined chart, under which payments increase over time. The payments are taxable in the year received. However the taxpayer can withdraw more than this as required.

As with RRSP payments, the amounts will qualify for the $1000 pension income amount on Line 314 if the taxpayer is over age 64 or receiving the amounts as the result of a spouse's death.

Before you withdraw, speak to your tax advisors about planning your income sources, including the following concepts:

- Equalizing income between spouses—who should withdraw first or most—the higher income earner or the lower?

- Can other income sources be split between spouses—Canada Pension Plan benefits for example?

- Should dividends be transferred from the lower earner to the higher earner (a possibility only if a Spousal Amount is thereby created or increased)

- Should one spouse be earning more or less interest, dividends or capital gains from non-registered sources to reduce family net income?

- How will the clawback of the Age amount or Old Age Security be affected by your pension withdrawals?

- How will your quarterly instalment payments be affected by your RRSP withdrawals?

- If you will be in a higher marginal tax bracket at death, should you withdraw more during your lifetime?

For information about RRSP accumulations at death, see Chapter 6.

CHAPTER SUMMARY:
ESSENTIAL TAX FACTS FOR WEALTH PRESERVATION

1. One of the reasons why today's Canadians are wealthier than generations before is that their financial assets include real estate and private pension accumulations.

2. You may wish to think of your capital accumulations within three primary categories:
   a. Tax exempt assets
   b. Tax prepaid assets
   c. Tax-assisted accumulations

3. When you withdraw money from an RRSP, both principal and earnings must be added in full to your taxable income, in the year of withdrawal, unless you withdraw under a Home Buyer's Plan or a Lifelong Learning Plan.

4. You can often use the tax system to create new capital without coming up with any new money, by "flipping" assets held in a non-registered account into an RRSP, thereby creating new tax savings.

5. The increase in value in capital assets held outside registered accounts will accrue on a tax-deferred basis until they are disposed of. Then, only 50% of the gains are taxable.

6. You might even own some tax exempt assets. . .for most households that includes one tax exempt principal residence.

7. Sometimes assets are sold to strangers or transferred to relatives. In fact, often assets can be transferred to spouses or children without immediate tax consequences.

8. The disposal of your assets can be through an actual sale or upon a deemed disposition.

9. When you transfer assets to your adult children during your lifetime, the property is always transferred at fair market value and tax consequences are immediately reported.

10. Capital losses may only be used to reduce capital gains in the current year. If losses exceed such gains, they may be carried back to reduce capital gains in any of the previous three years or in any subsequent year.

11. Gains on the disposition of personal use property are taxable, but subject to "The $1000 Rule".

12. In most cases, capital gains on disposition of the principal residence will be exempt from tax.

13. When a principal residence is used in part for business purposes (home office, child care enterprises, consulting, etc.) it is possible to retain the principal residence exemption as long as no capital cost allowance is claimed on the property.

14. When a commercial building is acquired, special reporting rules must be followed.

15. When a building is disposed of, the proceeds must be allocated to the land and building as well as other depreciable property.

16. On deciding whether a transaction is "income" or "capital" in nature, the courts have considered a list of individual circumstances.

17. It is CRA's view that the subdivision of farmland or inherited land in order to sell it will not necessarily constitute a conversion to inventory.

18. When you trade some of a group of identical shares, you must calculate an average cost each time there is a purchase.

19. Should a disposition of a qualified small business corporation share result in a capital gain, a lifetime capital gains exemption of $500,000 may become available.

20. Interest deductibility will hinge upon the direct and current use of money borrowed and the identification of an income-producing purpose.

NOW PUT MORE MONEY IN YOUR POCKET ALL YEAR LONG...

PERSPECTIVE

• Life can be like a game of "Snakes and Ladders" sometimes.

• Births, deaths, marriages, divorces, new jobs, severance, retirement, bonuses, insolvencies, terminal illnesses, inheritances. . .it is especially during times of great change that financial assets are in flux, and the tax consequences of their liquidation, transfer or changing values must be carefully addressed.

• Tough times or times of change are also the right times to review long and short-term financial priorities and the combined dynamics of new personal circumstances, market conditions and changing tax law. Why? You want to make informed decisions (or at least educated guesses) about your future, despite the uncertainty of change.

- While tax preparation is an activity based in history (the reconciliation of last year's tax obligations), tax planning aims to arrange a taxpayer's affairs within the framework of the law to minimize future tax obligations of the whole family unit.

- It's all about control, (which you have) in timing your capital dispositions throughout your lifetime, and at death. By taking charge, you can often influence the size of your after-tax return.

- Use the tough times to set yourself up for tax savings, now and in the future. Be sure to work with your tax and financial advisors to ensure you have maximized your tax filing rights in difficult times.

Remember: There are ten basic reasons why Canadians pay too much tax throughout their lifetime:

- They fail to diversify their earned income sources
- They pay too much to the government through tax withholding or tax instalments
- One person in the family earns significantly more than the others
- They don't maximize RRSP contributions
- They fail to build equity
- They have no long-term savings goals
- They have no estate planning goals
- They have trouble keeping records
- They have too much debt
- They only consider the tax consequences of their financial decisions at tax time.

A great way to address many of these pitfalls is to start a small business, the subject of our next chapter.

CHAPTER FIVE

ESSENTIAL TAX FACTS
FOR THE SELF EMPLOYED

Making the break to the freedom of self-employment? Good job!
To make a business work, it takes a great vision, relationships,
judgment, planning, perseverance, energy and most of all, the
ability to face and overcome failure. But in addition, you'll need
to do and know the numbers behind your business plan, and get
organized for a closer relationship with CRA—a reality for every
business owner. You'll need to know how to:

- Build wealth in a tax-efficient small business
- Audit-proof with retrievable records
- Manage a visit from the auditor
- Meet new Reasonable Expectation of Profit Tests
- Find and work closely with a competent tax advisor
- Classify deductible expenditures: operational and capital outlays
- Stay clear of non-deductible expenses
- Claim CCA on your capital assets
- Formalize the hiring of family members
- Use your business losses to your best advantage
- Maximize wealth: build income and equity with acumen
- Engage in personal tax planning for the small business owner

Build wealth in a tax efficient small business

Did you know that there are approximately 2.5 to 3 million unincorporated small businesses in Canada today, reporting net income of just under $40 billion? That's quite a vibrant business community. Yet, over the next 15 years, it is expected that the vast majority of businesses will change hands due to an aging demographic, and many of those have neither chosen a successor nor identified a cohesive plan for succession.

There is great opportunity here for a new generation of business owners, as well as those who will take the plunge from employment to self-employment as part of their pre-retirement plans.

The self-employed have the most flexibility, under the Income Tax Act, to maximize the time value of money to build significant after-tax wealth. There is, however, no doubt that compliance with the Income Tax Act is more onerous when you are self-employed. The "onus of proof" for numbers reported on the return falls squarely on your shoulders. However, you are aided by an Act which provides only general, rather than specific guidelines for income reporting and expense deductibility. That means you have the flexibility to write off a range of expenditures specific to your business enterprise, providing it is viable and you are prepared to justify what you report with hard and soft copy—that is, both receipts and reasons why your claims are reasonable under the circumstances.

Many small businesses start in home bases: unincorporated and run as one or two-person shops. This invites "mixed use" expenditures—those with both a business and a personal component—which must be properly accounted for. This is particularly true of home office, auto and entertainment or travel costs.

The Income Tax Act also provides generous tax cost averaging provisions. It acknowledges the risk entrepreneurs take in funding business start-ups first; reaping income and equity rewards later. In particular, it is possible to co-mingle proprietorship losses with other personal income of the year, thereby reducing overall taxes payable over several tax years. As you can imagine, this is a tax preference that can be lucrative, and therefore often challenged by CRA as to its reasonableness.

Incorporation may be a natural next step for a successful business, providing not only lower tax rates than the personal tax regime, but a way to build equity on a tax free basis. That's because qualifying small business corporations, can reap for their individual shareholders a $500,000 lifetime capital gains deduction upon later disposition. For a family of four adult shareholders—that represents a potential for $2 Million of tax exempt profits. . . not bad for the thousands of hours of unpaid labor, personal perseverance and financial risk borne by most small business owners.

Owner-manager compensation planning and family income splitting within a corporate structure allows for income diversification through the distribution of salary, dividends and capital gains to family members. Yet, this is not easy—successful business ownership requires more than the ability to produce top quality widgets—it takes disciplined business planning, astute marketing and customer service to survive and thrive throughout often unpredictable economic, personal and human resource hurdles.

In short, the self employed immerse themselves in the environment that maximizes the "pay yourself first rule." By controlling income source, when it's earned, who reports it and how much of it is subject to tax, you're in the driver's seat when it comes to creating after-tax wealth over a period of years.

How to audit-proof with retrievable records

Here's a big human resource tip for the newly self-employed: make sure the first person on the payroll is the bookkeeper. . .and that this person is meticulous and dedicated to detail and deadlines.

Even if you, the owner, have an affinity for debits and credits, your job is to grow the business, and ensure the books are kept so that you can make astute decisions based on accurate numbers. Your books are your roadmap—without a disciplined approach to business planning you risk driving off the main road, getting lost and driving in circles. What's more, the roadmap is required to pass compliance tests along the way, courtesy of CRA.

Essential TAX FACT #146

You are required under law to maintain proper books and records at your place of business to enable the taxes, payroll source deductions and GST/HST remittances to be determined, and these must be available for inspection by CRA. You must also file a tax return on time.

Should you file late, (the filing deadline is June 15 for proprietors), you will face the late filing penalties discussed in Chapter 1. Also know that if there is a balance due when you file, interest will be charged on that balance back to the normal filing deadline—April 30—so it pays everyone to file by April 30.

Should you file an appeal, records must be retained until any objection or appeal has been dealt with or the time for filing a further appeal has expired. CRA has the right by law to demand, either in writing or in person, that records continue to be retained beyond the six-year period. This usually happens if fraud is suspected.

Fed up with clutter? Taxpayers may request permission to destroy records before the six-year record retention period is up. To do so, the taxpayer must file *Form T137 Request for Deduction of Books and Records*. This may not be such a good idea as it is a direct invitation for CRA to audit the records prior to destruction. Remember, a person who destroys or otherwise disposes of records or books of account with the intent to evade tax could be subject to prosecution. See Chapter 1 for a summary of expensive penalties.

What must be kept? Just about any "source documents" related to your business activities: sales and purchase invoices, cash register receipts, formal written contracts, business plans, credit card receipts, delivery slips, deposit slips, memoranda, work orders, dockets, cheques, bank statements, tax returns, and general correspondence, and any other thing containing information, whether in writing or in any other form. These must be kept in a chronological, orderly manner.

CRA is also allowed to specify to a delinquent taxpayer, what records and books of account must be kept if the current books are found to be inadequate upon audit.

If the taxpayer fails to comply with record requests, it's serious. Maximum penalties are:

- a fine of not less than $1,000 and not more than $25,000

- both a fine and imprisonment for up to 12 months.

So, your investment in a reliable and meticulous bookkeeper will pay off. Expect to be asked for your tax records at some time during the life of your small business enterprise, be prepared to retrieve them with ease and be ready for questioning by filing an audit-proof return.

How to manage a visit from the auditor

Have you ever been audited? If so you'll know that the visit from CRA generally is preceded by letter, requesting specific information to justify figures on your tax return—such as moving, medical or child care expenses. In addition, the "normal reassessment period" for review of your files is three years: the current year and two years back. So you can expect to retrieve files for more than one year in most cases.

However, small business owners must be prepared to dig deeper and give more subjective information. Under our self-assessment system of taxation, you must meet the Onus or Burden of Proof and show a Reasonable Expectation of Profit exists in a commercially viable enterprise. This goes beyond the mere keeping of receipts.

Essential TAX FACT #148

Expenses claimed must be reasonable and incurred to earn income from a business that has a reasonable expectation of cumulative profit over a "profitability time period."

More on this later. Do note this also about the reporting of income: The tax department need not accept your return as filed, and can make a "Net Worth Assessment" on its own if you cannot explain the source of your income adequately. The Onus of Proof, in that case, is on you to prove otherwise.

For these reasons, you must remove any personal living expenses from business deductions. The best way to do this is to keep a log of business use compared to total use. Deposit income to separate business bank accounts and have separate credit cards for business/personal use.

When fraud is suspected by CRA, records can be requested beyond the normal reassessment period of three years. Know also that an authorized person employed by CRA may at all reasonable times come to inspect your books or examine your inventory.

Essential TAX FACT #149

Ask for it in writing! You have the right to see a written request for information and a list of issues to be answered. In addition, if the property in which you run your business is a dwelling, the person authorized by CRA may not enter it without your consent unless a search warrant is produced.

Essential TAX FACT #150

Keep copies of everything! The taxpayer also has the right to make copies of everything that may be seized by CRA, including electronic backups, which is something you should be sure to keep whenever you forward documentation to the CRA.

Under these rules, CRA auditors are also authorized to enter into any premises where any business is carried on, and in those circumstances, you must provide reasonable assistance and answer all proper questions.

However, the taxpayer does have certain rights, which you should know about and exercise.

The audit powers referred to above cannot be used if the inquiry is the subject of a criminal investigation.

It is also important to note that third parties approached by CRA are not required to provide information or documents related to other unnamed persons or third parties unless authorization has been given by a judge to obtain this information.

During a tax audit, you have the right to be present and to be represented by counsel throughout the inquiry, unless it is ordered otherwise. CRA would have to show that your presence would jeopardize the process. Likewise, those who act as witnesses, providing evidence in an inquiry, may be represented by counsel.

However, you must be nice: no taxpayer is allowed to physically or otherwise interfere with, hinder or molest an official of CRA.

Meet new reasonable expectation of profit tests

Any business that is legitimate for tax purposes is required to report, its "profit from that business or property for the year."

Profit is usually calculated according to the Generally Accepted Accounting

Principles (GAAP), however other benchmarks and methods have been accepted by the courts as well. For example, at times generally accepted rules of commercial trading are taken into account.

When it comes to business start-ups however, profits can be illusive, and this can be a challenge for taxpayers and their auditors. A business venture that is operated on a commercial basis for profit, may legitimately write off an operating loss for the fiscal period. This can be very lucrative.

In order for any amounts to be deductible on your tax return, you must be found to be "carrying on a business" within the fiscal period. So just when are you considered to have started the business? CRA's Interpretation Bulletin IT364 provides some guidance:

- A business starts whenever some significant activity that forms a regular part of the income-earning process takes place.

- There must be evidence of the type of business activity that will be carried on.

- An organizational structure must be in place to show whether this is a one-time transaction, or an on-going enterprise.

Next, build a framework for meeting tax filing obligations. Start by choosing a reporting period: for the majority of small businesses this is required to be the calendar year ending December 31. In some cases, an election can be made to select an off-calendar year end—providing there is a bona fide business reason to do so. You will need to select a method of reporting income.

Essential TAX FACT #151

An operating loss of the business can be used to offset all other income of the year, or, if an excess remains, all other income of the prior three years or the next 10 years, if the loss was incurred after 2003.

Essential TAX FACT #152

To determine a business start date, keep a detailed log of all business activities you have undertaken "for profit" as opposed to "for pleasure". It also will help to show how close you are to landing new contracts which will produce revenues.

Essential TAX FACT #153

Expenditures of the business must be connected or matched to income using the cash or accrual method of accounting on a consistent basis.

Under the accrual method, once an invoice has been rendered, it is included in the reporting of revenue, whether or not the cash has actually been received by the business. In other words, "accounts receivable" must be accounted for and included in income.

Expenses that the business has been billed for, but which are not yet paid, are deducted when calculating the income of the business. These are the "accounts payable" of the business.

The Income Tax Act requires the accrual method to be used in accounting for the income and expenses of a business. However, there are a few exceptions:

- farmers and fishermen may use the cash method (income is reported when actually received and expenses are reported when actually paid),

- certain professionals may report "Work in Progress" using a modified accrual method of accounting. This allows the professional to avoid paying tax on income that has not been billed for yet.

Finally, understand that your business expenses may fall into different categories for tax deductibility:

- **Deduction of Operating Expenses.** Operating expenses are also known as "business inputs" in GST jargon; or those expenditures that are necessary for you to produce the goods and services that bring in the revenues. These are items that are "used up," like supplies, advertising and promotions, rent, salary, communications costs, licences, etc. These items are usually 100% deductible in the fiscal year in which they occurred, unless there are specific restrictions in place. When gross revenues earned are reduced by operating expenses the result may be either net operating loss or an operating profit.

- **Deduction of the Cost of Depreciable Assets.** When you acquire an asset with a useful life of more than one year, you must classify that asset into prescribed classes set out in the Income Tax Regulations. Prescribed rates of amortization are claimed for those assets and the result is a deduction for Capital Cost Allowance or CCA. This subject is discussed in more detail later in this chapter. However, the key concept here is that you don't want to make the mistake of taking a 100% deduction for an expenditure that CRA is going to reclassify as a capital one. That can lead to expensive surprises later. It is also necessary to keep track of asset values on acquisition and disposition, whether or not a GST/HST rebate or input tax credit was received, an Investment

Tax Credit was claimed, or a special accelerated rate is available. Ask your advisor about these provisions.

- **Planning with CCA and Operating Losses.** The CCA claim also provides a series of tax-planning opportunities. For example, if operating expenses have already exceeded the gross revenues of the business, it may be wise not to take the CCA deduction in the current year and "save" a higher undepreciated balance for use in the future.

On the other hand, if the CCA deduction helps to increase or create a business loss that can be carried back to recover taxes paid in the prior three years, or the following ten years, the taxpayer may wish to maximize the claim. Such loss deductible can therefore be very valuable in recovering taxes previously paid or payable in the future.

In addition, by reducing net business income with CCA, you may be able to save money on your CPP liability come April 30. This is significant for businesses in which net profit is just over $40,000.

Essential TAX FACT #154

To allow you to deduct your business losses, your CRA auditor requires you to demonstrate a profit motive in the venture.

If a business clearly has a commercial basis, and there is no personal element to the business write-offs, the courts have recently ruled that the taxpayer is considered to have a legitimate source of income, and therefore losses cannot be denied by CRA, if they are reasonable. This is so, even if there has never been a profit, and may never be any.

Essential TAX FACT #155

It is proposed that a limit will be placed on any losses from a business or property unless it is reasonable to expect the taxpayer will realize a cumulative profit for the period in which the source of income is earned and the business or property is held, or in which the taxpayer can reasonably be expected to carry on the business or hold the property.

However, in response, the Department of Finance has since introduced proposed legislation to disallow losses from a business or investment unless it provides income from a "source"—that is, income from a business or property that has a reasonable expectation of profit over a "profitability period".

If passed into law, this new test will apply to taxation years after 2004. Small business owners must be prepared to show, for each year a business or investment shows a loss, it is reasonable to assume that the business or

Essential TAX FACT #156

Capital gains are not included in the calculation of annual or cumulative profit from a business. What this means is that operational losses will not be allowed in spite of the fact the investment is expected to result in a capital gain on later sale.

investment will generate a cumulative profit over the "profitability period". Once allowed, the losses will not be disallowed, even if the business never makes a profit.

But, it is in the year the taxpayer ceases to carry on the business (or sells the investment), the other shoe drops: the "profitability period" ends and a test for cumulative profit is made. Losses in the final year will be limited to the cumulative profit from that business or investment.

You should ask your tax advisor to keep you informed on the status of this legislation, as it will have an important effect on the kind of records you must keep. The wise taxpayer and tax advisor will ensure that the following is available for audit starting in 2005:

- Hard copy of income, expense and capital outlays
- Business plans including cash flows, marketing, human resource and capital acquisitions
- Projections for income from the business for the next 5 years

Therefore, if this is not yet obvious, new audit requirements above should help you come to the conclusion that, for the small business owner, it is critical to find the right tax advisor.

Find and work closely with a competent tax advisor

Working with the right tax advisor can be one of the most profitable long-term professional relationships in your lifetime, especially when you consider the time and energy you might need to expend on a future tax audit. Your tax advisor can be your mentor and business partner.

But just how do you find a trusted, intelligent, and knowledgeable tax advisor who clicks with you? Consider the following checklist in your search:

- **Seek Referrals:** Ask your friends and business associates for referrals
- **Research Sources:** The yellow pages, local newspapers, professional

associations and Chambers of Commerce or Boards of Trade in your area all are sources of information.

- **Interview Three:** Always interview at least three different advisors from varying backgrounds and firm sizes to ensure their services and your needs match. You might consider a commercial tax preparation service, a large accounting firm, a financial planner or an independent, designated accountant. It's best to include one from every group to get the best overview of potential service, quality and price. You will receive a broad sampling of services and fees and, most important, an opportunity to judge the effectiveness of communications with you.

- **Qualifications.** Enquire about the potential advisor's ability to speak to other clients about their experience with this person. Also find out how the professional updates his or her knowledge in taxes from year to year.

- **Ask About Fees and Service.** Don't ever be afraid to ask about fees, guarantee of service, billing practices, errors or omissions insurance, and what the fees for service cover. What happens when errors occur? Who is responsible, who covers the costs? Is assistance with follow-up on Notice of Assessment or future audit work included in the fee?

- **Is this a pro team player?** Is this professional able and willing to interact with others in your pro advisory team: lawyers, financial planners, insurance advisors and so on? This should be a requirement.

- **Get Help Defining Needs.** Have the candidates help you define your needs; then ask them to help you find the level of expertise required to meet the following needs: annual tax preparation, corporate as well as personal returns, trust returns and estate planning, bookkeeping, accounting, auditing and financial planning.

- **Ask Your Top Three Tax Questions.** Be prepared to go through a formal and consistent interview process. Ask your top three tax questions or concerns of each candidate as a starting point, and make notes of their answers.

- **Listen Well.** When you ask your questions, take note of the way the answers are communicated to you.
  - Can you learn from this person?
  - Is the person willing to help you learn?
  - Is the person interested in you and your business?
    - Does s/he make suggestions to you?
    - Does s/he have a strong background in taxation?
    - How do you feel? The last thing you need is an aura of intimidation

or unclear communications. This is your business, your money. You are looking for peace of mind and a professional partner for the future of your business and personal affairs.

- **Make the Decision.** Choose the advisor you are most comfortable with.

Once you have made your selection, begin the relationship by:

- Reviewing prior-filed returns, for at least the previous 10 year period, to make sure you haven't forgotten to claim a tax deductible item on your federal return
- Communicating your personal financial planning goals, as well as your business objectives, in the immediate year and within the next three years.
- Asking your advisor to help you keep current on tax changes from an individual, investment and estate-planning point of view.

Classify deductible expenditures: operational and capital outlays

To make more of your business expenditures tax deductible, ensure that there is a source of income or a potential for an income source in the future; match expenses to income and classify operational and capital expenditures properly.

Remember: Operational costs are usually 100% deductible; some expenses, however, may have restrictions placed on them; others could be non-deductible. See the following common expenses. Variations thereof should be discussed with your tax advisor:

Accounting and Legal Fees. All taxpayers may deduct legal and accounting fees or expenses for advice or assistance in preparing, instituting or prose-cuting an objection or appeal in respect of:

- an assessment of tax, interest or penalties under the *Income Tax Act* or a similar provincial law,
- a decision of the Canada Employment and Immigration Commission, the Canada Employment Insurance Commission, or a board of referees or an umpire under the *Unemployment Insurance Act or the Employment Insurance Act,*

- an assessment of income tax, interest or penalties levied by a foreign government or one of its political subdivisions if a foreign tax credit is available for those taxes
- an assessment or decision under the Canada Pension Plan or a similar provincial plan.

Accounting fees paid for auditing, planning, tax compliance, bookkeeping and other accounting advisory services can be deducted.

Commission salespeople and self-employed taxpayers can deduct the cost incurred to prepare their tax returns. In addition to the cost of preparing their returns, accounting fees paid for auditing, planning, bookkeeping and other accounting advisory services can also be deducted.

For example, legal fees on the purchase of a building for a business are not deductible. Legal fees in these cases are included as part of the capital cost of the asset, and form part of the CCA class balance.

Canada Pension Plan. Proprietors must make their own contributions to the Canada Pension Plan (CPP). This is often quite a shock at tax filing time, especially to new business owners whose net income is around the $40,000 mark.

Essential TAX FACT #157

The deductibility of legal fees depends on the activity that gave rise to the fees. Legal fees that arise from the normal operations of a business are deductible. For example, fees charged by a lawyer to perform annual business filings are deductible. So are fees charged by a lawyer to take collection proceedings on overdue accounts. But, legal fees that arise from capital transactions are not deductible.

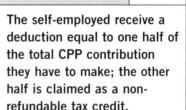

Essential TAX FACT #158

The self-employed receive a deduction equal to one half of the total CPP contribution they have to make; the other half is claimed as a non-refundable tax credit.

The CPP contribution is based on net self-employment earnings and at the time of writing was set at 9.90% of the net amount, indefinitely. Self-employed individuals must pay both the employee and employer portions of CPP. At its maximum level this contribution is well over $300 a month.

Convention expenses. To be deductible, a convention attended by the taxpayer must be related to the business, and be reasonable as to location. For example, a doctor in British Columbia would not likely be able to deduct the cost of a fly-fishing convention in Montana. An exception might be possible, however. If the doctor specialized her practice in the area of allergies there may be some argument that the convention would be business related if several potential clients or specialist speakers attended the event.

However, costs paid for a guest to accompany a taxpayer to a convention are not deductible. Unless the guest is actively involved in the taxpayer's business, the guest's attendance would be considered by CRA to be personal in nature, and therefore not deductible. Also see Seminars and Training later.

Credit card and airline points use. It is very common for a self-employed taxpayer to use a personal credit card with some form of "reward miles" for business expenses. The business then reimburses the taxpayer so the card balance can be repaid. The use of the credit card, and the subsequent repayment, pose no problems per se.

Health Care Premiums. Health care premiums paid on behalf of family members employed in the business will be a deductible expense where income earned from self-employment activities is a taxpayer's main source of income. As these enterprises often employ family members, it is important to note that after 1997, equivalent deductibility is extended to non-arm's length employees, but with a restriction. In order for premiums to be deductible as a business expense, they must also be paid for arm's length employees.

If the amount actually paid exceeds these limits, the excess may be included as a medical expense when the taxpayer calculates the personal medical tax credit.

Note that premiums paid for mandatory provincial health care plans will not be deductible. These amounts are paid by all taxpayers, and are not considered to be incurred in order to earn business income.

Interest Expense. Interest costs on borrowing to finance business operations will be deductible if they are based upon a legal obligation to repay the principle amount of the borrowed funds. Compound interest will also be deductible and if the taxpayer refinances lending arrangements, the replacement loan will be treated as if it were the original loan.

Leasing Costs. Tax treatment of the cost of leases in a small business falls into two different categories.

- *Operating Leases.* This type of lease provides the right to use a certain asset for a specific period of time. At the end of this time, the asset may be returned to the lessor, or purchased for a price that

approximates fair market value at that time. Lease payments paid on an operating lease are fully deductible providing the asset has a business purpose. If the lease is for a passenger vehicle, the lease expense is limited to $800 per month.

- *Capital Leases.* This type of lease can take many forms, but it always transfers ownership of the asset to the lessee, at the end of the lease term, or allows the lessee to purchase the asset for an artificially low price (a bargain purchase). In other words, this type of lease is basically a form of financing a purchase, even though it is called a lease.

Interest costs that are imputed in the lease are also deductible, but may be

Essential TAX FACT #162

In recent court cases, the courts have ruled that the direct use of borrowed funds is the primary determinant of the whether or not the interest is deductible. So you must be prepared to trace the use of the funds directly to an income-earning potential and remove any personal use component.

Essential TAX FACT #163

When it comes to the tax consequences of capital leases, the lease payments are not deductible. Rather the asset is capitalized, and applicable CCA rules and rates are applied.

subject to a monthly restriction if the taxpayer drives a luxury or "Passenger Vehicle", discussed in further depth later in this chapter.

Seminars and training. Training costs can be classified as "capital" in nature if they provide a lasting benefit to the taxpayer. This may include the acquisition of a new skill or qualification. However, if training is taken to maintain, update or upgrade an existing skill, the costs are 100% deductible. The only exception to that rule arises when the amounts are being claimed as a non-refundable tax credit. In that case, they can't also be used as a deduction on the business statement.

Essential
TAX FACT #164

Any costs of training that are personal in nature are not deductible. If training is taken abroad, or in conjunction with a personal holiday, for example, the costs may be disallowed, particularly if similar training is available here in Canada.

Essential
TAX FACT #165

Professionals are allowed to deduct their WIP at year-end, where the revenue has been recorded as gross revenue. When WIP was deducted at the end of the previous taxation year, it is added to gross revenue the next taxation year, and that year's ending WIP is deducted.

The following expenses of training are 100% deductible:

- Courses taken to maintain professional standards
- Courses taken to provide content in field of expertise
  (e.g. a tax course by an accountant)

Training expenses that are capital in nature, forming an addition to the Cumulative Eligible Capital Account, include courses that that result in a degree, training to be a specialist, diploma or professional qualification.

Remember: when it comes to training and adjacent holidays, food and lodging will not be allowed for personal holiday time, but expenses incurred on the date of arrival and date of departure will be considered deductible. If training costs are really conventions, the taxpayer will be limited to the "two per year" rule.

Work in Progress. Work in Progress (WIP) refers to a professional's time, which has not been billed yet. For example, an accountant working on a large audit might accrue time that will be billed once the work is completed. At any point in time prior to billing for the audit, the value of the accrued time is considered WIP.

Professionals eligible to deduct their WIP include accountants, dentists, lawyers, medical doctors, and veterinarians.

There are two other types of expenses to discuss at this time:

- Non-deductible or restricted expenses
- Capital expenditures

Stay clear of non-deductible expenses

"But I thought my golf membership dues were deductible, honey—CRA now wants my tax refund back—with interest!" Make sure this scenario doesn't happen to you! Be on the lookout for the following expenditures which are not deductible when you file your income tax return, and ask your tax and financial professionals about them:

- **Advertising.** No deduction for expenditures made in foreign print or foreign broadcast media is allowed on the Canadian tax return unless the advertising message is directed primarily at the Canadian market. Note that foreign periodicals are generally exempted from this non-deductibility rule. Provided that 80 percent or more of the periodical's non-advertising content is original, Canadian businesses will be able to deduct 100 percent of their advertising costs, without regard to whether or not it is directed at the Canadian market. If the periodical cannot meet the 80 percent criteria, only 50 percent of such advertising costs will be deductible.
- **Club Dues for Yachts, camp, lodge, golf course**
- **Fines and penalties.** Fines or penalties imposed after March 22, 2004 by any level of government (including foreign governments) will not be deductible under the Income Tax Act. Three exceptions to this new rule, which will be known as "prescribed penalties" are:
  - Interest penalties under paragraph 110.1(a) of the Excise Act
  - the Air Travellers Security Charge Act (subsection 53(1) of the Air Travellers Security Charge Act.)
  - the GST/HST portions of the Excise Tax Act.
- **Legal and Accounting Fees.** Generally, legal and accounting fees are allowable deductions where they are incurred in connection with normal business activities, transactions or contracts incidental or necessary to the earning of income from a business or property. They will not be deductible, however, *if they are incurred on behalf of a capital*

disposition. (The outlays of legal costs must instead be added to the capital cost of the asset in that case).

- **Life Insurance Premiums.** Life insurance premiums, in general, are not deductible to a company when the company is the beneficiary of the policy.

  When life insurance is required by a lender, the lender is a commercial financial institution and if the interest on the loan the lender provides is deductible the premiums would be deductible to the company.

  Note: Only the net cost of pure insurance is deductible in situations where universal and whole life policies are used.

  Where a company is not the beneficiary of a policy the amount may be deductible under ordinary rules, i.e. where an employee or employee's family are beneficiaries of a policy and the policy is provided as a taxable fringe benefit to the employee.

- **Membership fees or dues to dining, sporting, or recreational facilities.**

  Note: there is no prohibition against deducting the cost of legitimate entertainment expenses incurred in such facilities, subject to the 50 percent limitation on meals and entertainment explained below.

- **Meals and Entertainment:** Expenditures for food, beverages, or entertainment are restricted to 50% on the tax return. Entertainment includes all activities with a recreational component. For example, tickets to the World Cup of Hockey for a key customer would be considered entertainment.

  The following costs for meals and entertainment can be claimed in full:

  - *Fundraising Events.* Expenses incurred during the course of conducting a fund-raising event for a registered charity.

  - *Reimbursed Meals and Entertainment Expenses.* The most common situation is where "out-of-pocket" expenses are charged to a client who pays them along with their regular bill. These expenses are only deductible in this case if they are fully disclosed on the invoice rendered to the client. (the client, however, is restricted by the 50% rule when they claim these expenses).

  - *Taxable Benefits.* Meals and entertainment costs that are included as a taxable benefit to an employee. For example, an employer purchases a set of season tickets to a sporting venue, and assesses the employee a personal benefit on their T4 slip at the end of the year. The employer would be able to fully deduct the cost of those tickets. If this employee was eligible to deduct meal and entertainment expenses on their tax return, they would be entitled to deduct entertainment expenses where they actually entertained clients with the tickets – limited by the 50% restriction.

– *All Employee Events*. Expenses that are incurred as a benefit for all the employees of a business are deductible. Usually this takes the form of special events such as Christmas parties, staff picnics, barbeques, etc. Up to 6 such events may be held in a fiscal year, and avoid the 50% restriction.

· **Restricted Automobile Expenses.** For a number of years, it has been the policy of the government to discourage business use of what it perceives to be luxury automobiles. This has been accomplished by limiting the amounts that can be deducted for Capital Cost Allowance (CCA) and interest on automobiles that are owned by the business, as well as by limiting the deductibility of payments made under leasing arrangements. The history of these maximums appear below—as you can see annual adjustments are possible but not automatic.

Fixed expenses are based on certain maximums as outlined below:

Date	Interest Costs	Leasing Costs	Capital Cost
Jan. 1 to Dec. 31, 2000	$ 8.33 a day	$ 700 a month plus taxes	$ 27,000 plus taxes
Jan. 1 to Dec. 31, 2001 to 2005	$ 10.00 a day	$ 800 a month plus taxes	$ 30,000 plus plus taxes

This restricted "passenger vehicle" classification can be avoided, if the vehicle is used more than 50% of the time to transport goods or equipment (in the case of a pick up truck) or 90% of the time in the case of a van. Such vehicles are known as "Motor Vehicles."

Hence the Auto Log. This is a document (paper or electronic) that records distance driven for two purposes: *personal use* includes the use of your car by other family members, driving kids to hockey or dancing, driving

Essential TAX FACT #166

If you buy a Mercedes for use in your business for $95,000, be aware that your capital cost allowance deduction will be based on a maximum capital cost of $30,000 plus taxes, as it is considered to be a luxury or passenger vehicle.

grampa to the eye doctor, picking up milk, lunch with personal friends or relatives, etc. *Business use* includes driving to and from appointments, picking up mail or office supplies, but not driving to and from your place of business or employment.

"But I always claim 100% and I've never been challenged!"

I'm sure you've heard this line, too. But, this unsuspecting taxpayer is quite possibly next in the audit queue! In practice, very few 100% claims are allowed under the auto expense line item when a return is picked for audit. I have seen a couple in my experience in practice over the years, however, in each case, the taxpayer was able to show, definitively, that one car (or other mode of transportation) was used exclusively for personal matters and one only for employment/business.

For example: Sophia, a self-employed commissioned salesperson, who has an auto log, finds that of the total 15,000 kilometres she drove in the year, 5,000 were for personal use. Total expenses for the year include her leasing costs of $400 per month and operating costs of $3500. Her deductible claim is computed as follows:

(10,000 / 15,000) * (4,800 + 3,500) = $5,533.

Tips on Keeping the Auto Log. If you are like most people, and have trouble keeping the log, try this: take a moment at the end of each day to log distance between appointments in your manual or electronic day calendar. And at the start and end of every month take a moment to jot down the numbers from your odometer.

Claiming CCA on your capital assets

No one really knows for sure what the value of an asset is at any given point in time. This will only be realized upon disposition — when the owner sells the asset, or disposes of it in another way — like converting it to personal use or transferring it to a relative, for example. However, for tax purposes, an income-producing asset used in a business can be "written down" to acknowledge depreciation due to its use.

This is really an educated guess. The Department of Finance has eliminated some of that guesswork by prescribing special classes and rates your depreciable property will fall into. Depreciable property is any property you will be claiming a special deduction on for tax purposes, called "Capital Cost Allowance" or CCA. CCA is a deduction calculated on a CCA schedule, which is taken at your option to reduce your business income.

The CCA schedule will require the charting of the following information:

Any undepreciated capital cost (UCC) balance from the previous year: If you made a claim for CCA last year, you will be carrying forward an Undepeciated Capital Cost at the beginning of this year. Reduce this balance by any GST Rebate you may have received for an auto or musical instrument last year.

The cost of new acquisitions: Here you will record the capital cost of an income-producing asset you started to use for business purposes during the year and any significant improvements to its useful life during the ownership period. In the case of passenger or luxury vehicles, that capital cost will be limited to $30,000 plus taxes under current restrictions. (See further explanations below). Other adjustments may be necessary in cases where properties are transferred amongst related or affiliated persons.

The proceeds of disposition: What is required here is the reporting of the lesser of two figures:

- the actual proceeds of sales or *fair market value* in cases where assets are transferred or disposed of without the change of money and
- the capital cost of the asset. The limit to the capital cost of the asset is necessary in cases where the disposition results in a capital gain—an increase in value over capital cost. The capital gain portion of the

disposition will be reported on Schedule 3 of the tax return.

The result is the base amount for the CCA claim: UCC at the beginning of the year plus cost of additions less proceeds of disposition. If the amount in this column is negative, a "recapture" of CCA is necessary. This means you have essentially overstated the depreciation of your assets and the negative amount is added to income.

If the amount here is positive and you still own assets within the CCA class, do continue to make your CCA claim under normal circumstances—that is, at your option. However, if you no longer own any assets in the class and a positive amount remains, you'll claim a deduction for a "terminal loss" if you are self employed. If you are an employee, terminal loss claims are not allowed.

Essential TAX FACT #169

A "half-year rule" is applied to your CCA claim for most assets. That is, in the year of acquisition, the normal CCA rate allowed can be applied only to half the cost of the asset for most assets.

There is one more adjustment you need to know about and this one is important in terms of your decision-making regarding acquisition dates for additions to your capital asset pool.

Classes and Rates. The tax recognition given to your depreciating assets, known as CCA, is calculated using a "diminishing-balance method." This means that a fixed maximum percentage is applied against the balance of the capital cost of the asset remaining at the end of each year. To arrive at this fixed percentage, assets of a similar type are classified or "pooled" into specific classes for CCA purposes. You will find a complete list in Schedule II of the Income Tax Regulations 1100-1102. But, for your information, we have included some basic rates and definitions for common assets you may be investing in:

Class	Description	CCA rate
1	Most buildings made of brick, stone, or cement acquired after 1987, including their component parts such as electric wiring, lighting fixtures, plumbing, heating and cooling equipment, elevators, and escalators	4%

Class	Description	CCA rate
8	Property that is not included in any other class such as furniture, calculators and cash registers (that do not record multiple sales taxes), photocopy and fax machines, printers, display fixtures, refrigeration equipment, machinery, tools costing $200 or more, and outdoor advertising billboards and greenhouses with rigid frames and plastic covers	4%
10	Automobiles (except taxis and others used for lease or rent), vans, wagons, trucks, buses, tractors, trailers, drive-in theatres, general-purpose electronic data-processing equipment (e.g., personal computers) and systems software, and timber cutting and removing equipment	20%
10.1	Passenger vehicles costing more than $30,000 if acquired after 2000 ($27,000 if acquired in 2000; $26,000 if acquired after 1997 and before 2000)	30%
10(f)	Electronic equipment acquired before March 22, 2004 and equipment acquired after March 22, 2004 but before 2005 for which the separate class election under Reg. 1101 is made.	30%
45	Computer equipment acquired after March 22, 2004 other than equipment acquired after March 22, 2004 and before 2005 for which the separate class election is made under Reg. 1101.	45%

Circling back on some key definitions and concepts for claiming your CCA deduction, it is important to note the following:

*Deemed dispositions or transfers are valued at **Fair Market Value (FMV)**;* that is, the highest dollar value a willing buyer, unrelated to a willing seller, would pay for the asset on the open market. There are special rules when the amount received for the asset is inadequate, especially between related parties, when trade-in values are below FMV or if assets are disposed of at a superficial loss. Ask your tax advisor about these circumstances.

Repairs or Improvements. Does the repair of an asset add to its useful life? If so, the amounts are likely added to the capital cost of the asset, rather than written off as an expense in full. Does the repair, on the other hand, simply put the asset back to its original condition? In that case, we generally write off the costs in full. In another example, replacing the shingles that blew off the business premises during a windstorm would be fully deductible, whereas replacing the whole roof would be treated as a capital expenditure.

Short Fiscal Years. The CCA claim is generally prorated when there is a short fiscal year. This means that if you started your business on July 1, and had a December 31 fiscal year end, only 50% of the normal available CCA deduction allowed can be claimed. If you started your business on September 1, only one third of the normal CCA deduction is claimable, and so on.

**Essential
TAX FACT #170**

Even though small pieces of equipment and supplies may have a useful life of more than one year, if their value is under $200, they can generally be written off as operating expenses. Examples of such items are calculators, pencil sharpeners and desk lamps. However, if they form part of a set (like sales signs used by a real estate agent) the total cost of the set of like depreciable items must be considered and added to the cost base.

**Essential
TAX FACT #171**

The taxpayer can choose to capitalize any annual financing fees paid for the assets, simply by adding the cost on to the undepreciated capital cost of the asset, in order to preserve more of those costs for future use, when profits are perhaps higher. To do so, the taxpayer must make an election under Subsection 21(3) of the Act.

Reminder on Asset Transfers or Dispositions. You might want some professional help when it comes to handling your asset dispositions. Always remember to tell you advisor when you have sold depreciable assets or transferred them to personal use or to an employee or relative. Deemed dispositions will require an appraisal of the asset's fair market value at the time of disposition.

Special Rules for Autos. How you claim CCA for a vehicle will depend on whether it is considered to be a "motor vehicle" or a luxury or "passenger vehicle" for tax purposes.

Motor vehicles will not be restricted as to their capital cost, leasing or interest costs. They include vehicles costing less than $30,000 plus taxes.

Motor vehicles are scheduled in Class 10 in one CCA "pool" of assets. When a vehicle in Class 10 is sold, the proceeds from selling it are used to reduce the remaining CCA balance in the pool of assets.

Class 10.1, on the other hand, is used to house individual passenger vehicles—one vehicle per class. In other words, the purchase or disposition of one of the Class 10.1 vehicles has no impact on the other Class 10.1 vehicles you may own.

Each is restricted to a maximum capital cost of $30,000 plus taxes under current rules. However, make the determination on whether your asset belongs in Class 10.1 based on its cost *before* taxes. Besides the normal "half year" rules on acquisition of the vehicle, there is a second "half year" rule on disposition. No further terminal loss write-offs or recapture are allowed.

Closing of Business. If a taxpayer ceases to carry on a business, no claim for a terminal loss is allowed for the depreciable property that was used in the business unless and until all the assets in a class are disposed of. This would be the case where the taxpayer retains the property after the close of business, without using it for any other purpose. Neither may the taxpayer claim CCA on the property in any subsequent year unless it is used in that year to earn income from a business or property. If the taxpayer commences to use the property for a non-income-producing purpose, there is a deemed disposition of the property at that time at its fair market value.

Such a deemed disposition could result in a CCA recapture or a terminal loss.

Adjustments. If your return has not yet been assessed, CRA will normally allow a request for an adjustment to your CCA claim and results on your return, so it is important to act immediately if you notice an error or omission. If you have already received a Notice of Assessment for the current year, follow the same procedures and contact the tax department as soon as possible for a revision. In practice, revisions

Essential TAX FACT #172

CCA is known as a "permissive deduction." The claim is made at the taxpayer's option, however, CRA is not bound to adjust prior filed returns under the Fairness Provisions, which currently allow a ten year period to adjust errors or omissions on prior filed returns for most other federal tax provisions. Instead, the taxpayer must know to manage the CCA accounts within certain time frames and notify the CRA promptly if an error is made or a revision is required.

and the changes to the results on your return may be allowed, however, CRA is not required to change the outcome on the return once your appeal rights, based on the date of filing of a Notice of Objection, have passed. In those cases adjustments may only be accepted if they do not result in a change to the outcome of the return filed. So, if you want to change the results on your return with your CCA claim adjustments, do so within the required time lines.

Essential TAX FACT #173

A Notice of Objection must be filed within the later of 90 days from the date on your Notice of Assessment or Reassessment or one year from the due date of your return.

In the case of statute-barred years, CRA will consider requests to change your CCA schedule on a case-by-case basis, but will apply those changes generally only if the results on the return remain unchanged. So this will allow you to make certain changes to the UCC in the class, for example, but not to claim more CCA to reduce taxes payable.

Planning with CCA Claims: Here are the top ten Essential Tax Facts you should discuss with your tax advisor regarding your income-producing assets:

1. **Discuss your Notice of Assessment or Reassessment from CRA with your tax advisor upon receipt.** Changes you wish to make to your claims for CCA have a time limit: adjustments can only be made within 90 days of receipt of the Notice of Assessment or Reassessment.

2. **Never claim capital assets as operating expenses.** 100% write-offs are not allowed on the purchase or improvement of assets with a useful life of more than one year. This is an expensive mistake that can cost you money.

3. **Schedule the cost of improvements to assets.** Restoration of the asset to its original condition is deductible. The cost of improving the asset is generally capitalized.

4. **Classify your assets correctly.** Make sure you know the CCA rate that will be applied to the new asset you are thinking of purchasing, and whether there is an exception for the half-year rule.

5. **Prorate your CCA claim in the first year of business.** CCA rates and the half-year rule apply to businesses that are in existence for a full fiscal year. This means that a business that started mid-way through a fiscal year must prorate the calculated CCA claim by the number of days the business was operating.

6. **Consider capitalizing the interest costs if your business is losing money.** This is a great way to preserve the costs for use in the future when income may be higher.

7. **Consider the effects of disposing of all the assets of a class.** Recapture will increase your net profits; terminal losses will decrease them. Do some tax planning to assess proper tax timing of dispositions, if this makes sense otherwise (i.e., the buyer is co-operative).

8. **Be aware of special tax provisions for asset purchases.** The government often provides tax incentives for those who invest in new assets in their business. Check out the latest interpretations of recent federal and provincial budget provisions with your tax advisor before purchasing new assets.

9. **Track GST/HST paid carefully.** If you are a GST/HST registrant, you'll be able to claim back the cost of your taxes paid on the asset against your GST/HST remittances. This can give your cash flow an important boost, so don't forget to give this information to your tax advisor. Complete the CCA tracking system suggested in Figure 5.1 to make sure all the information you need to properly file your income tax return as well as your GST/HST return is available.

10. **Always prorate your maximum CCA deduction for any personal use of the asset and bring details of your asset acquisitions and dispositions** to your tax advisor each and every year. This includes what happened during the tax year, as well as previous asset tracking worksheets.

Formalize the hiring of family members

It is common for a small business owner to hire family members. When you hire family members in your business you'll need to define whether the relationship is one of employment (master-servant) or sub-contracting (contract for service). Also, amounts will only be deductible if they were incurred to earn income from a commercial venture, reasonable under the circumstances and actually paid for work actually done.

Employee or subcontractors? Check out Chapter 2 for Essential Tax Facts surrounding an employer-employee relationship. If you or a family member works as a "subcontractor" you are considered to be self-employed, and the business which hires you on is not required to make statutory source deductions on your behalf. CRA defines a business relationship to be the following:

"a verbal or written agreement in which a self-employed individual agrees to perform specific work for a payer in return for payment. There is no employer or employee. The self-employed individual generally does not have to carry out all or even part of the work himself. In this type of relationship, a *contract for service* exists."

The amounts invoiced to the business must be paid in a timely fashion to the sub-contractor (usually within 30 days). By the way, the invoiced amount is fully deductible by the business owner. If you hire your family members to work in your business—that's you.

Essential
TAX FACT #174

When you hire family members in your business you will need to know whether the relationship you have is a contract of service or a contract for service. This will help you determine whether you will be required to make statutory deductions to stay onside with CRA.

The subcontractor who is unincorporated must then remit CPP premiums via the income tax return at year end, and in some cases, tax instalment payments, quarterly. In addition, if the subcontractor earns more than $30,000 in gross fees billed, GST/HST registration may be required. This should be taken into consideration before deciding on what status your family member prefers to have in working within your business.

There are four basic factors CRA will look at if the determination of your employee's status is borderline:

1. **Control.** The degree of control exercised by the payer will help to define the relationship with the person doing the work. If the payer has the right to hire or fire, controls the payments of wages and how much is to be paid, and decides on the time, place and manner in which the work should be done, including hours of work, and the assessment of quality of work, generally there is a strong indication of an employer-employee relationship. Additional factors include control of the list of clients of the business and the territory covered, as well as training and development.

2. **Ownership of Assets and Tools.** If the payer supplies the equipment and tools required to perform the tasks of the job and pays for repairs, insurance, rental, fuel or other costs of operation, generally an employer-employee relationship is considered to exist.

3. **Risk of Loss.** The payer is generally considered to be the employer if

s/he assumes the financial risk for the company including the responsibility for covering operating costs like office expenses, salaries, insurance coverage, freight and delivery, rent, bad debts, damage and promotional expenses. Those who receive remuneration without financial risk — that is, salary is paid in full regardless of the health of the business — would generally be considered to be an employee.

4. **Integration.** This final factor is considered from the worker's viewpoint. If the worker is not dependent on the payer, and simply integrates the job done for the payer into his own business activities, the worker is likely self-employed. It would be important to show that the self-employed person has other jobs lined up with other suppliers, for example, to consolidate this position. However, if the job done for the payer is actually integrated into the payer's commercial activities, to the extent that the worker is connected with the employer's business and dependent on it, likely an employer-employee relationship exists.

Taken all together, the circumstances surrounding these four criteria will generally help you to determine whether an employer-employee relationship exists.

In addition to the Employment Insurance premiums and Canada Pension Plan contributions withheld from the employee's paycheque, the employer must also contribute to these plans. The employer must contribute 1.4 times the EI premium deducted, and must match the CPP contribution deducted. The gross wages paid to an employee are deductible expenses for a business. In addition to this, the employer's share of EI premiums and CPP contributions are also deductible. However, amounts withheld from the employee's pay for tax, EI, and CPP and remitted to CRA are not deductible expenses.

Essential
TAX FACT #175

An employer pays employees an agreed-upon wage, less mandatory statutory deductions for Income Tax, Employment Insurance, and Canada Pension Plan contributions. These deductions must be remitted to CRA monthly. Penalties come into plan when you misclassify the status of your workers or remit late or deficiently.

Essential
TAX FACT #176

Proprietors should also know that no deduction is available for drawings taken from their business. They are taxed on net income of the business before their drawings. However, it is possible to deduct (on line 222) one-half of the total CPP premium payable on the net business income.

Small Business Source Remittances. Employers with average monthly withholding amounts of less than $1,000 for the second preceding calendar year and who have no compliance problems in either their withholding account or GST/HST account, for the preceding 12 months, may choose to remit their source deductions on a quarterly rather than a monthly basis, on March 31, June 30, September 30 and December 31. The remittances are due the 15th of the month following the end of each quarter.

Use your business losses to your best advantage

The tax system in Canada allows for an effective way to average out the highs and lows business cycles. Small business owners may write off business losses from a proprietorship against other income of the year.

Non-capital losses that cannot be absorbed by other income in the year incurred may be deducted against other income in any of the previous three years or the following seven years (losses incurred for taxation years ending before March 23, 2004) or ten years (losses incurred for taxation years ending after March 22, 2004). Losses not claimed at death or in the carry over years, simply expire.

Essential TAX FACT #177

Non-capital losses include losses from employment, business, and active partnerships. They are deducted on Line 252 of the tax return.

Essential TAX FACT #178

Any farm loss will be limited to 100% of the first $2,500 of loss, and then 50% of any remaining farm loss, to a maximum of $8,750 if the farming enterprise is not the farmer's chief source of income.

Losses from a commercial farming operation are a specific form of non-capital loss that contain a variation, when farming is not the chief source of income. In that case, only a "restricted farm loss" may be deductible.

Restricted farm losses will offset any other sources of income. If the actual farm loss is greater than $2,500, the excess may be carried back three years, or forward for ten years to offset net farm income realized in those years. Restricted farm losses not claimed at death or after ten years expire.

There is an exception to the rule, however. If the farm loss was created or increased by interest costs or property taxes on the farmland, these costs may be added to the cost base of the land and used later upon disposition to decrease any gain. However you can't use these costs to create or increase a capital loss on the sale. Ask your tax advisor about these rules before you sell the farm.

Also explore the following with your advisor:

- *How do we Maximize Non-refundable Credits?* Your Basic Personal Amount and most other non-refundable credits cannot be carried forward—use them or lose them. So claim only enough losses to reduce the taxable income to the value your non-refundable credits.

- *How do we avoid higher tax brackets?* If the taxpayer's taxable income is normally above the upper limit of the lowest tax bracket it may also be advisable in some cases to claim only enough of the available losses to reduce the taxpayer's income to that limit and save the remaining losses to claim in other years.

- *What type of losses are deductible first?* Listed personal property losses and restricted farm losses should be deducted first as they must be applied against specific income sources. Use up oldest non-capital losses first and be mindful of expiry dates.

- *Can CCA be used at my Option?* Yes. It may make sense to forego the CCA deduction and claim non-capital losses to ensure that they do not expire. However, this may effect the size of your refundable and non-refundable tax credits.

Build income and equity with tax acumen

Make income and a profit. . .that's what most small business people are focused on in their day-to-day affairs.. In the background however, something even more powerful is happening with small businesses that grow. . .equity is being built for the owner and his/her family. Problem is, so many entrepreneurs fail to anticipate just how quickly their businesses can take off—often attracting potential buyers along the way.

If you were approached to sell your business tomorrow, would you be ready to sell? Would your tax structure be opportune? This is something that should be discussed with your advisor. The opportunity to create serious wealth in the future is often enhanced by taking advantage of the Lifetime Capital Gains Exemption.

Essential TAX FACT #179

The Income Tax Act provides for unique tax treatment upon the disposition of certain investments in the shares of a Qualified Small Business Corporation (QSBC) or a qualified farm property. Should that disposition result in a capital gain, a lifetime capital gains exemption of $500,000 may become available.

The capital gain from the sale of a qualified business is reported in the first section of Schedule 3 and the resulting Capital Gains Deduction (CGD—this is 50% of the Capital Gains Exemption of $500,000) is claimed on *Form T657*. The CGD is available to taxpayers who own shares in a qualifying small business corporation, or a qualifying farm property. Specific rules of eligibility must be met, however, before the claim for the deduction can be made.

Qualified Farm Property. The available CGD must be reduced by any CGD previously claimed. Contact CRA for a record of previously used amounts. The definition of "qualified farm property" that was acquired after June 17, 1987, includes real property owned by the taxpayer, spouse or child for at least 24 months immediately before sale. Also, a gross revenue test must be met; that is, in at least two years prior to disposition, gross income earned by the individual from active farming operations, must exceed net income from all other sources. Third, all or substantially all of the fair value of the farm assets must be used in active business operations for at least 24 months prior to disposition.

Different rules exist for farms acquired before June 17, 1987. The CGD will be allowed, but only if the farmland and buildings were used in an active farming business in Canada in the year of sale or in at least five years during the period the property was owned. For 1988 and subsequent tax years, eligible capital property (for example, farm quotas) will constitute qualified farm property eligible for the deduction if used in the course of carrying on the business of farming in Canada.

Qualifying Small Business Corporations. To qualify for the CGD, the shares of the SBC must be:

- Shares of a small business corporation that was owned by the taxpayer, spouse or common-law partner, or a partnership related to the taxpayer,
- The corporation must be actively using at least 90% of its assets (on a fair market value basis) in the operation of the business,

- During the 24 month period prior to the disposition, at least 50% of the corporation's assets (on a fair market value basis) were used in an active business carried on primarily in Canada,

- During the 24 month period prior to disposition the shares were shares in a Canadian controlled private corporation.

In particular, check out these holding and purification requirements with your tax advisor and find out how family income splitting can be enhanced with the ability to maximize CGD during a taxpayer's lifetime.

Once an entrepreneur, always an entrepreneur! If a taxpayer disposes of a capital property used in a business (a former business property) and replaces it with another property, it is possible to elect that any gain on the sale of the former property be deferred until the replacement property is disposed of.

> **Essential TAX FACT #180**
>
> Know that even if you sell your business, it is possible to defer your capital gains into the future, if you decide to take the plunge again on a second venture.

Deferral of recapture of CCA and eligible capital property is also possible, but such a tax deferral is only applicable if a replacement property is acquired within specific time frames:

- Involuntary Dispositions —the replacement property be acquired before the end of the **second** taxation year, after the one in which the disposition occurred.

- Voluntary Dispositions —the replacement property be acquired before the end of the **first** taxation year after the year in which the disposition occurred.

If it is necessary to acquire more than one property to replace a former business property then each of the properties acquired is considered to be a replacement property.

Speak to your tax advisors well before your sign on the dotted line to sell your company. In particular, make sure that your non-compete clauses are structured to enable you to tap into these special tax deferral opportunities.

Engage in personal tax planning for the small business owner

A major tax planning consideration for any owner manager is whether to incorporate or not. Aside from liability issues, which should be discussed with your legal advisors, the answer is often one of timing, use of start up losses, and diversification of compensation to family members who work in the business.

For example, you may wish to earn start-up losses in a proprietorship, in order to offset other income of the year — perhaps from a severance package. Or, if there are excess losses, you may wish to carry them back and offset employment income earned in the best of the last three tax years, or take advantage of carry forward opportunities, which allow you to use excess non-capital losses to offset other personal income in the next 10 years. You will also want to be conscious of your opportunities to create and maximize RRSP contribution room, which you can do inside or outside of the corporation..

Incorporating your proprietorship could have several key tax advantages:

- The opportunity to design a compensation package for shareholders, who are also employees, that may encompass employment income, as well as the distribution of dividends from the company's after-tax profits.

- The opportunity to utilize the $300,000 small business deduction to reduce corporate tax rates.

- The opportunity to earn tax-free capital gains through the use of the $500,000 Capital Gains Exemption.

The decision to pay a salary or take some other form of remuneration such as dividends from a corporation should be carefully discussed with your tax advisors, in particular to explore a number of key factors which drive this decision:

- To be deductible to the corporation an owner manager's salary has to be reasonable.

- Salary is deductible to the corporation; dividends are not.

- Salary qualifies as income eligible for RRSPs; dividends do not.

- Salary qualifies as income for purposes of Canada Pension Plan contributions; dividends do not.

- Salary can create additional costs to the corporation with respect to the employer portion of CPP contributions, employer portion of Employment Insurance premiums (if the owner manager does not own more than 40% of the voting shares of the corporation) and the potential for provincial payroll taxes.

- Salary which is declared but unpaid must be paid within 179 days after the end of the taxation year in which the expense was incurred. If the amounts are not paid, the expense in the corporation is denied, resulting reductions in taxes and interest owing on the income in that corporation.

- Payment of a salary requires the corporation to withhold income taxes from the amount. Payment of a dividend does not have this requirement unless the payment is made to a non-resident owner manager.

- Provincial tax integration can also play a role in an owner manager's decision of whether to take salary versus a dividend.

- Dividends are a positive addition to the Cumulative Net Investment Loss account (see *Form T691*) which affects a taxpayer's ability to claim the Lifetime Capital Gains Exemption; salary is not.

Therefore, when preparing the income tax return of the corporation it is important to either "bonus down" or "salary down" compensation expenses to the small business limit. That is because the integration between the corporate and personal tax systems will only work when the corporation is paying tax at small business rates. After that, there is a significant cost to paying high rate taxes in the corporation and then a dividend personally to the shareholder.

Essential TAX FACT #181

The business limit for small business deduction purposes is $300,000 for 2005 and subsequent years. After 2004, because of the general rate reduction, all income above the small business deduction limit is taxed at the same rate.

Family RRSP Maximization. Your tax advisor should review the following RRSP planning opportunities with you:

RRSP Deduction Limit – note the maximum earned income requirements to maximize RRSP contribution room are 18% of earned income to the following dollar maximums:

Year	Maximum	Earned Income Required in Prior Year
2003	$14,500	$80,556
2004	$15,500	$86,111
2005	$16,500	$91,667
2006	$18,000	$100,000

After 2006, the limit will be indexed by increases in the average industrial wage. In planning for salary versus dividend income, always try to maximize earned income for RRSP purposes first, and then payout dividends. These strategies should be developed for each family member working in the business.

CHAPTER SUMMARY:
ESSENTIAL TAX FACTS FOR WEALTH PRESERVATION

1   The self-employed immerse themselves in the after-tax environment that maximizes the "pay yourself first" rule.

2. By controlling income source, when it's earned, who reports it and how much of it is subject to different marginal tax rates, you're in the driver's seat when it comes to creating significant after-tax wealth over time.

3. Compliance with the Income Tax Act is more onerous for the self-employed, who can expect to be audited more frequently because of their requirement to "self-assess."

4. The Income Tax Act provides generous tax cost averaging provisions by allowing the co-mingling of proprietorship losses with other personal income of the year.

5. Owner-manager compensation planning and family income splitting opportunities abound for the small business owner, particularly because income can be diversified through the distribution of salary, dividends and capital gains to family members.

6. Big HR Tip: the first person on the payroll should be the bookkeeper.

7. You must store income tax records and receipts until six years after the end of the tax year to which the records relate.

8. Expenses which are reasonable and incurred to earn income from a business that has a reasonable expectation of cumulative profit over a profitability time period will be allowed and resulting operating losses will be deductible.

9. An operating loss of the business can be used to offset all other income of the year, or if an excess remains, all other income of the prior three years or the next 10 years, if the loss was incurred after 2003.

10. Expenses of the business must be connected or matched to income using the cash or accrual method of accounting on a consistent basis.

11. Business expenses may fall into several categories for tax deductibility including the deduction relating to business operations and deductions relating to the acquisition of depreciable, and non-depreciable income-producing assets.

12. Working with the right tax advisor can be the most profitable long-term professional relationship in your lifetime—prepare a checklist for finding the most knowledgeable, trusted advisor.

13. Several expenditures are restricted for tax purposes (meals and entertainment) or non-deductible (club dues for golf courses). Discuss these in advance with your advisor.

14. If you buy an expensive passenger vehicle for use in your business, be aware that your capital cost allowance deduction will be based on a maximum capital cost of $30,000 plus taxes.

15. CCA is known as a "permissive deduction". The claim is always made at the taxpayer's option in order to promote tax planning opportunities.

16. When you hire family members in your business you'll need to define whether the relationship is one of employment (master-servant) or sub-contracting (contract for service). Also, amounts will only be deductible if they were incurred to earn income from a commercial venture, reasonable under the circumstances and actually paid for work actually done.

17. Should the disposition of a qualifying small business corporation or qualifying farm result in a capital gain, a $500,000 lifetime capital gains exemption is available.

18. Know that if you sell your business, it is possible to defer your capital gains into the future if you decide to take the plunge again on a second venture.

NOW PUT MORE MONEY IN YOUR POCKET ALL YEAR LONG...

PERSPECTIVE

Have you ever wondered how millionaires are created in Canada? Recent statistics tell us that currently about 1% of Canadians are millionaires now and that this number is expected to triple in the first decade of the new millennium.

Half of our millionaires have come upon their good fortune through inheritances. Others have become wealthy through the sale of their capital assets, such as their small business corporations.

Will your family be among those who become millionaires in the next several years? Remember, it takes just as much time and effort to think big as it does to think small. When you think big, on tax savings, that is, you will have a very good chance of joining the ranks of Canada's top wealth accumulators.

But, let's begin at base point. Tax planning is an activity we typically think of reserving for high-income earners. But in reality, tax planning is for everyone at every income level who is interested in accumulating significant wealth. While earnings certainly factor into this, more important is your focus on capital accumulation and appreciation. The investment in a small business can help in this regard, as you build both taxable earnings for each family member, and equity within the enterprise itself.

For the small business owner, minimum family tax-planning activities should include the following strategies :

- How can we maximize the use of each family member's Tax Free Zone?

- How can we diversify income source to produce the best after-tax results?

- How can we best split income earned by the family, and share the capital appreciation within the business?

- How do we maximize each family member's RRSP contribution room to create tax sheltered pensions?

- How do we minimize "Realized Income for Tax Purposes" and defer tax into the future?

- How do we best invest outside the corporation to avoid having all eggs in one basket?

- How do we maximize social benefits, including future employment insurance and CPP benefits for family members?

- How do we avoid the "kiddie tax" or "Tax on Split Income" on the returns of minor children?

- How can we set up our affairs to utilize each family member's $500,000 Capital Gains Exemption?.

CHAPTER SIX

ESSENTIAL TAX FACTS
FOR SINGLES AND SENIORS

"Singlehood" may, in fact, be responsible for much of the complexity within our Income Tax Act today. It may also become the great catalyst for tax change tomorrow, as baby boomer demographics bring a new paradigm to the fore. This chapter is about change—the transition in and out of singlehood for some— and its tax consequences:

- Tax preferences available to singles
- Managing tax advantages of your first job
- Leveraging investments: Pay down the mortgage or contribute to the RRSP?
- Love and marriage: integrate tax planning into new conjugal relationships
- Sudden singlehood: planning tax-wise exits
- Single parents and their dependants
- Singles who give care to dependant adults
- New rules for claiming medical expenses
- Preparing for death and widowhood

To make better economic decisions, it is important to understand your own concept of "self-actualization" and its timeline in your life, especially if you are currently single.

Anyone who took an introductory psychology course in college may remember Maslow's Hierarchy of Needs. This gentleman identified "self-actualization" as the highest state of human satisfaction. The self-actualized individual is free of the pursuit of basic needs. This person can enjoy the world around him or her without fearing uncertainty in the future. The achievement of this blissful state, however, involves planning and choices.

At a high level, personal money management begins with an analysis of your needs and desires, and a motivation to put a series of plans into place throughout your lifetime to meet those needs. Once primary needs are satisfied—food, clothing, shelter—an understanding of what motivates us to act further in planning our financial destiny is necessary.

Tax preferences for single taxpayers

Tax and the single taxpayer. . .the best way to look at this phenomenon is along life's highway. The young and single need to focus on tax advantages unique to their age group:

- Your first post-secondary degree or diploma
- Your first job
- Your retirement savings
- Your first home
- Your first conjugal relationship
- Your mobility—tax deductible moving

After life's firsts, come life's transitions: to every thing, there is a season:

- Separation or divorce
- Single parenthood
- Your second and subsequent post-secondary degrees or diplomas
- Caregiving for adult family members
- Death and taxes

Before delving into the tax specifics of some of the issues above, you'll need to know the following: if you are single, affluent and don't have dependants, you will often bear the full burden of progressivity within our tax system—that is, the more income you realize, the higher your tax bracket and tax rate and the more you will pay—usually with the benefit of only one personal tax credit, instead of several within a family household. You may, however, qualify to take advantage of certain tax preferences: deductions, income-tested tax credits and social benefits, depending on your personal circumstances, as summarized below:

Tax preferences available to singles, with no dependants

Deductions:

- Registered Pension Plan and RRSP contributions
- Union or professional dues
- Disability supports deduction
- Business investment losses
- Moving expenses
- Support payments
- Carrying charges
- Other deductions on lines 222 to 256 of the tax return

Refundable tax credits:

- Federal GST Credit
- Provincial Refundable Tax Credits
- Refundable medical expense supplement
- Refund of investment tax credits
- Employee and partner GST/HST rebate

Non-refundable tax credits:

- The basic personal amount
- The age amount if you have attained age 65 in the year
- CPP and EI contributions
- Pension income amount (if you are receiving qualifying superannuation)
- Disability amount
- Amount for interest paid on student loans
- Tuition and education amount
- Medical expenses
- Donations and gifts

When you add dependants to the mix, singles may also qualify for the following tax preferences:

Deductions:

• Child care expenses

Refundable tax credits:

• Federal and provincial Child Tax Benefits

Non-refundable tax credits:

• Amount for eligible dependant (formerly known as equivalent to spouse amount)
• Amount for infirm dependants age 18 or older
• Caregiver amount
• Disability amount transferred from dependant
• Tuition and education amounts transferred from a child
• Medical expenses for other dependants

The actual dollar amounts assigned to these provisions can change every year, due to indexing or the introduction of new measures in government budgets. Check out recent figures in *Essential Tax Fact Sheets* available at www.knowledgebureau.com, and discuss current changes with your tax advisor:

What happens when others want to split income with singles? First, know that all the normal Attribution Rules discussed in prior chapters will apply to transfers between related parties.

Singles must also be mindful of the Attribution Rules surrounding their gifts to minors. For example, Sonia, a single 40 year old, wants to give her 10-year-old niece, Jamie a $10,000 cash gift for investing purposes. Resulting interest, dividends, or royalties will be taxed in Sonia's hands. However, resulting capital gains are taxed in the hands of Jamie.

Elizabeth, a 48-year-old widow, on the other hand, wants to gift her 10 year

---

Essential TAX FACT #183

Singles who live alone will be unable to split income with other dependants in the traditional sense, but they may give gifts to those within their family circle. When that happens the Attribution Rules may still apply.

old nephew, Vincent, who lives in Europe, a $10,000 lump sum for investment purposes. In that case, there are no Attribution Rules, as Vincent lives abroad.

When it comes to their investments, singles need to look after "No. 1"—they need to minimize the tax they pay on current earnings, and learn discipline in savings strategies even if they are mobile. They can own one tax exempt principal residence, and that's a good place to starting investing.

With other asset choices, they must focus on whether to defer taxable income to the future and how to diversify realized income sources year over year. Therefore, whether you are a single senior or junior, you will be wise to work with three key tax savings opportunities:

- *Protect earned income from tax erosion:* The best way to shelter current earnings from employment or self employment is with the RRSP, which provides immediate tax savings and a tax deferral on investment income. But it is only available to those who are age eligible (under 70) and who have RRSP contribution room. For those over 69, continued tax sheltering in a Registered Retirement Income Fund (RRIF) or other annuity remains an option.

- *Earn tax efficient pension income sources.* There are few tax shelters for pension income—the government basically wants their tax dollar now—after providing years of deferrals to accumulators.

The pension income amount of up to $1000 provides relief though. Who qualifies? Those who are:

   – **Age 65 or older** and in receipt of pension payments from superan-

Essential TAX FACT #184

When adults pass assets or money to other adults who are not related, there is generally a disposition at fair market value and tax consequences in the hands of the giftor. The acquirer records the fair market value of the property as the adjusted cost base on their books.

Essential TAX FACT #185

Seniors may be in a lower tax bracket during their lifetime than at death. If this is so, discuss RRSP withdrawal options with your tax advisors. Also consider your gifting strategies to other family members or intentions for charitable giving.

Essential TAX FACT #186

A tax credit of up to $1000 may be available under the pension income amount on Line 314.

nuation, taxable portions of foreign social security (less exempt amounts deducted on Line 256), annuity payments from an RRSP, RRIF, Deferred Profit Sharing Plans (DPSPs)

- **Under age 65** and in receipt of periodic pensions as part of a life annuity, taxable portions of foreign social security payments. Annuity payments from an RRSP, RRIF, Deferred Profit Sharing Plans (DPSPs), will only be eligible if received as a result of the spouse's death.

- **Move with tax caution.** Remember that the provincial taxes you pay will be determined by your province of residence on December 31. If you are moving from a province that is taxed at lower rates than your next one, consider moving at the start of next year. If you move before December 31 all income of the current year will be taxed at the new province's higher tax rates. Remember to check out a detailed list of moving expenses in *Essential Tax Fact Sheets* at www.knowledgebureau.com.

- **Be even more careful moving in.** Conjugal relationships can bring both positive and negative tax changes, including the following.

  - **On the positive side:** the opportunity to claim a spousal amount, transfer age, disability, pension or tuition and education amounts, equalize CPP benefits, split dividend income (providing a spousal amount is increased or created by doing so), split other investment income sources (being mindful of the Attribution Rules), make a spousal RRSP contribution, and co-mingle medical expenses, political contributions or charitable donations to obtain a better net family claim.

  - **On the negative side:** the co-mingling of family net income will reduce claims for refundable credits, the loss of the amount for eligible dependant. Also, one principal residence will become the taxable one, as a family unit can only own one tax exempt principal residence, etc.

Managing tax advantages of your first job

Feels good to have some cash, doesn't it? Most young singles don't realize that the time in life when you will have the most disposable income is often when you are a dependant, living at home and working at a good job. This is the time you should be saving, rather than spending. . .be sure to make a detailed list of Christmas and birthday wishes so that the other adults in your life can deal with non-deductible consumer spending needs on your behalf.

It pays handsomely to conform to four basic rules when you land your first job:

- Decide how much you are going to save and stick to this rule (50% if you can manage it is a great minimum number if mom and dad are paying your living costs)

- Always file a tax return to build unused RRSP contribution room and tap into your GST Credit at age 19 (as a minimum file a tax return when you are 18 to tap into this)

- Always make your maximum RRSP contribution, based on available RRSP contribution room, when you become taxable (you can contribute before this and earn tax-deferred investment income, if you like, just save your deduction until later)

- Never overpay your taxes at source—make sure your employer is withholding the right amount of Income Tax, CPP and EI but no more. Remember that those who are under 18, over 70 or in receipt of a CPP benefit, don't need to contribute to the CPP. Those whose income is under $2000 will also qualify for a refund of EI contributions.

The following income sources often earned by young singles also require special attention:

Waiter, Bartenders and Tips. If you work in the service industry as a waiter/waitress, bellhop, taxi driver, etc. be sure to record tips received and report the amount on Line 104 of your income tax return. You may receive them in cash, but keep a log of your earnings, as audits are common in the hospitality industry. Without a daily record, the CRA may disagree with your income figures and increase them to the amount they decide they should be. . .especially if they audit the restaurant or check what your colleagues have been reporting as tips. You may elect to pay CPP contributions on your reported tips by filing *Form CPT20.*

Essential TAX FACT #187

Report your tips or risk facing an expensive tax audit.

Essential TAX FACT #188

Employed apprentice mechanics may qualify for a tax deduction for the cost of their tools; unfortunately other mechanics will not.

Cost of Mechanics Tools. The cost of tools acquired by employed mechanics are generally not deductible, however a special rule exists for new tool costs of apprentice vehicle mechanics. Those who are enrolled in an educational program leading to a designation as a licensed motor vehicle mechanic may deduct, starting in 2002, the cost of tools acquired against the income made in their employment as an apprentice. If those costs exceed income, the amounts can be carried forward to a subsequent tax year. The deduction will be limited to the total cost of the tools and ancillary equipment required for the apprenticeship and the greater of $1,000 and 5% of the individual's income for the year from the apprenticeship.

Essential TAX FACT #189

Students in receipt of scholarship, fellowship or bursary income may qualify for a tax exemption of up to $3000.

Essential TAX FACT #190

Unused student loan interest may be carried forward for use by the student for up to 5 years.

Essential TAX FACT #191

Education Assistance Payments from RESPs are taxable to you when withdrawn. This will increase your net income, which could affect the size of your GST Credit and other provincial tax credits. You may wish to make an RRSP contribution to offset this.

Students and their Scholastic Rewards. If you are in receipt of a scholarship, fellowship or bursary, the first $3000 received may be tax exempt if you otherwise qualify to claim an education amount. See Fact Sheet at www.knowledgebureau.com for details. If you don't qualify for the education amount, you'll be able to claim a $500 exemption. Similar prizes obtained through your employment, however, will not qualify for any exemption. But if you are in receipt of a research grant, report only the net amount (amounts received less out of pocket expenses) on your tax return.

Remember to transfer any unused tuition and education amounts to your supporting parent, grandparent or spouse and to track any unused student loan interest costs for carry forward purposes (this non-refundable credit can only be claimed by the student for prescribed student loans made under the Canada Student Loans Act, the Canada Student Financial Assistance Act, or similar provincial or territorial government laws for post-secondary education. Unused claims can be carried forward for five years.)

Leveraging investments:
Pay down the mortgage or contribute to the RRSP?

When you buy a home, you will generally be taking a giant step towards wealth creation. This investment has the potential to provide you with:

1. Tax exempt capital appreciation

2. A hedge against future inflation

3. A possibility to produce income (from rentals or home office use)

4. Equity that can be leveraged to acquire other income-producing assets

Buying a home, can however provide some real risk as well. Besides the taxes you pay throughout your lifetime, the acquisition of a mortgage can be your most significant lifetime debt. The risk of loss is also present, especially if you have to move because you lost your job, were transferred, are getting divorced, or find the renewal of your mortgage term brings with it substantially higher—and unaffordable—interest costs.

To make matters worse, losses on the sale of your personal residence are not tax deductible (although if you must sell because your employer requires you to move, the employer may be able to cushion your losses on a tax free basis. See the discussion of tax free benefits in Chapter 1).

**Essential
TAX FACT #192**

While capital gains enjoyed on the sale of your principal residence are not taxable, losses incurred are not tax deductible, either.

**Essential
TAX FACT #193**

The cost of interest paid on your home mortgage are generally not tax deductible unless the home is used for an income earning purpose by a self employed individual.

Also significant is the fact that interest costs are usually non-deductible (however, if you use the home as an income-producing property, you may be able to write off a portion of those costs. See Chapter 4 on revenue properties and Chapter 1 on home office expenses of the employed or self employed.). Therefore you need to carefully manage the repayment of mortgage principal (the quicker the better) and mortgage interest payments (the lower the rate the better). Consider the following in your discussion on wealth creation and preservation with your advisors:

COMPARISON OF COSTS WITH VARYING DOWN PAYMENTS

$100,000 Home; 9% Interest Rate, Increased Down Payment of $25,000

Down Payment	Amortization	Monthly Payment	Total* P & I	Interest Only	Saving
$25,000	25 Years	$620.99	$186,297	$111,297	
$30,000	25 Years	$579.60	$173,880	$103,880	$ 7,417
$50,000	25 Years	$413.99	$124,197	$ 74,197	$37,100

*Principal and interest

By increasing your down payment by $25,000 up front, you'll save $37,100 in interest costs over 25 years.

COMPARISON OF COSTS WITH DIFFERENT AMORTIZATION PERIODS

Down payment of $25,000 on a $100,000 home, 9% interest rate

Amortization	Monthly Payment	Total P + I	Interest Only	Savings
25 years	$620.99	$186,297	$111,297	
15 years	$753.39	$135,610	$ 60,610	$50,687 over 25 years
10 years	$943.42	$113,210	$ 38,210	$73,087 over 25 years

By amortizing your mortgage over 10 years instead of 25, you will save close to $75,000 more towards your financial independence.

COMPARISON OF COSTS WITH INCREASING PAYMENT FREQUENCIES

$100,000 Home, $75,000 Mortgage at 9%, Original Amortization: 25 Years

Payment Frequency	Amount of Payment	Amortization	Interest	Savings
Monthly	$620.99	25 years	$111,297	
Accelerated Weekly*	$155.25	19.3 years	$80,642	$30,655

* Your monthly payment divided by 4 reaps significant tax savings by lopping almost 6 years off your amortization period. So if you can't afford a large down payment, compensate by paying your mortgage off every week instead of monthly.

Finally, your mortgage interest rate is the next most significant factor in managing your costs. The next chart shows how 1% or 2% differences in rates can multiply your cost savings:

COMPARISION OF COSTS WITH VARYING INTEREST RATES
$100,000 Home, $25,000 down payment; $75,000 Mortgage

Rate	Amortization	Monthly	Total* P + I	Interest Only	Savings over 10% rate
7%	25 Years	$525.32	$157,596	$ 82,596	$43,665
8%	25 Years	$572.42	$171,726	$ 96,726	$29,535
9%	25 Years	$620.99	$186,297	$111,297	$14,964
10%	25 Years	$670.87	$201,261	$126,261	n/a

* Assumes same rate and monthly payment throughout full amortization period.
  Figures are estimated.

COMPARISON OF COSTS WITH PREPAYMENTS OF PRINCIPAL
Original Amortization Period: 25 Years; on $75,000 mortgage at 9%
Prepayment of 20% of Mortgage in each of 5 years

Year	Monthly Payment	Balance Principal	Amortization Months	Interest Paid	Total Interest on life of mortgage
1	$620.99	$75,000	300	$6593	$111,297
2	620.99	$59,313	166	$5226	$ 50,364
3	620.99	$45,670	107	$4110	$ 32,595
4	620.99	$33,862	70	$2817	$ 25,536
5	620.99	$23,382	45	$2204	$ 23,309

Here the result is that after the first five years, you have produced interest savings of $87,988 over what would have been paid under a 25 year amortization period. Not bad!

Obviously, the decision to buy your first home requires careful consideration around the level of your down payment, interest rates and monthly repayment schedule, which can make tens of thousands of dollars of difference to you in the long term. All of these factors should be discussed with your real estate professional, tax professional, lawyer and financial institution.

But the burning question is this: how can I accumulate enough savings to do all of this in the first place? Your tax refund is a good place to start!

Assume you are in a 42% marginal tax bracket, and you contribute your maximum contribution to an RRSP this year, which your Notice of

Assessment states is $12,000. Making the contribution will save you $5040 on your tax return.

Now you take a look at your mortgage picture. Assume you will apply your tax savings, which you are receiving monthly because you have requested a reduction of taxes withheld at source, to your mortgage. This equates to $420 a month. If you have a $100,000 mortgage, currently amortized over 25 years, at an interest rate of 9%, you would be paying approximately $828 a month. If you bumped this payment up by $420, you'd cut your amortization period by almost 15 years. (monthly payments of $1258 on a $100,000 mortgage at 9% will pay it off in 10 years).

Therefore by making your annual RRSP contribution you will afford you the following opportunity:

1. Accumulate tax sheltered earnings from principle of $12,000 for ten years. At a compounding rate of 9% this would grow to $198,724

2. Save 15 years on your mortgage amortization.
   25 years x $828 x 12 months   = $248,400
   10 years x ($828 + 420 = $1248) x 12 months   = $149,760
   Difference   98,640

3. Total accumulations by making annual RRSP
   contributions of $12,000
   and investing them in the home mortgage
   over a 10 year period   = $297,364

The numbers speak for themselves!

Love and marriage:
integrate tax planning into new conjugal relationships

**Essential
TAX FACT #194**

You are considered to be spouses for tax purposes when you are legally married.

When you fall in love, and your single life turns to couplehood, it can be one of the most rewarding events of your life, not only for your emotional well being but also for your financial strength

To start, your new living arrangements can generate a claim for the spousal amount. The spousal amount, and the spouse's net income thresholds, change every year due to indexing. See www.knowledgebureau.com for more information. Provisions relating to the spousal amount, relate equally to common-law partners. In each case, we are referring to unions between the same or opposite sex.

So when does one enter a conjugal (rather than platonic) living arrangement with a spouse for tax purposes? First, and simplest, is the act of legal marriage.

It is possible that you will be able to claim a "spousal amount" for your new wife or husband in the year of marriage, but this will be based on their net income (Line 236) for the whole year, no matter when you get married —even December 31!)

If you are choosing to live as common-law partners, you will be treated the same as spouses for tax purposes if you live together as at the end of the year and you have a natural or adopted child together. Or, if not, once you have lived together for a continuous period of 12 months and in that time have not separated for more than 90 days you will attain common-law partner status.

It is also important to note that no taxpayer may make the spousal amount claim in respect of more than one spouse or common-law partner in the year and that only one individual may make the claim in respect of the other individual.

Essential TAX FACT #195

If the spouses or common-law partners are living apart at the end of the taxation year, then only the spouse's income for the period while the couple were living together is used in the calculation of the spousal amount.

Essential TAX FACT #196

If one spouse is required to pay spousal support for the other spouse, in the year of change, the payor may either claim the spousal amount or take the deduction for spousal support paid, but not both.

Essential TAX FACT #197

In the year of death, the spousal amount may be claimed in full on the final return and on any of the optional returns filed for the deceased.

Where two (or more) individuals are qualified to make the claim in respect of another, then those two individuals must agree who will be making the claim or neither will be allowed the claim.

Non-Resident Spouses. In order for an individual to claim the amount for a spouse or common-law partner for a non-resident spouse it is necessary that this person be supported by or be dependent on the taxpayer. The question of support or dependency is determined on the facts of each case. If the non-resident spouse or common-law partner has enough income or assistance for a reasonable standard of living in the country in which they live, they are not considered to be supported by or be dependent for support on the individual.

To support a claim for a non-resident spouse or common-law partner, an individual has to provide proof of the amounts paid or given as support of the spouse or common-law partner.

Single parents and their dependants

Whether you are a single parent by choice or circumstance, the tax system delivers three primary tax preferences to a single parent, which you should look into immediately after when a new baby is born:

- *Refundable credits:* Child Tax Benefits and GST Credits
- *Non-refundable credits:* Claims for the amount for eligible dependant
- *Deductions:* claims for child care expenses

In addition, you should plan to save for your child's education immediately by tapping into generous tax-assisted savings provisions under the Registered Education Savings Plan (see Chapter 3). As a minimum, try to save the Child Tax Benefits received in a separate account in the name of the child—resulting investment earnings will be taxed to the child rather than the parent and therefore will accumulate on a tax free basis.

Claiming your tax credits. Both the federal and provincial governments provide tax credits to certain taxpayers to promote social and economic policy goals.

So just how do you claim these credits? The answer to the question is a bit mystical, as the majority of taxpayers have difficulty actually finding them on the tax return! Non-refundable tax credits are found on Schedule 1.

Refundable tax credits are calculated automatically by CRA—so you don't normally see any forms or apply in any way to receive these credits, other than by filing your personal income tax return.

Another point of confusion for tax filers is how tax credits differ from tax deductions. Non-refundable tax credits provide equal benefits to all taxpayers, whereas tax deductions benefit taxpayers in higher tax brackets more than taxpayers in lower tax brackets. However, both refundable and non-refundable tax credits are determined in conjunction with a net income-based means test. That is, some credits are "clawed back" when income exceeds a certain pre-determined level, thereby phasing out benefits to higher income earners. Unfortunately, this results in higher marginal tax rates for those within "clawback zones" than for the highest income earners.

Also note that non-refundable credits found on Schedule 1 are of no benefit to those with no taxes owing. They are based on the individual's net income, or the net income of that person's dependants.

Essential TAX FACT #200

Tax Credits are tax preferences which are deducted from taxes owing or in some cases refunded to the taxpayer, even if no taxes are owing. It is therefore important to understand your rights to "non-refundable" or "refundable" credits.

Essential TAX FACT #201

Every dollar invested in an RRSP or other deduction which reduces net income, reaps a higher marginal benefit for low to middle income earners than for some high income earners.

Essential TAX FACT #202

Refundable tax credits will benefit even those with little or no income—they are a redistribution of income through the tax system. So you don't have to have income to receive them, but you must file a return to report family net income on Line 236— that is, your own income and that of your spouse or common-law partner.

The Child Tax Benefit. This federal refundable tax credit is composed of the National Child Tax Benefit plus two supplements, the National Child Tax Benefit Supplement for lower-income families and Child Disability Benefit for families with disabled children. Certain provinces and territories also offer child benefit and credit programs administered by CRA.

The CTB is paid each month to an eligible individual for a qualified dependant, who is a person who was:

- under 18

- not claimed as a spouse or common-law partner by another individual

The recipient of the benefit must also:

- Reside with the qualified dependant

- Be the parent who is primarily responsible for the care and upbringing of the qualified dependant (the female parent who lives with the child, is generally considered to be that person)

- A resident of Canada or the spouse or common-law partner of a resident of Canada

Essential TAX FACT #203

Once eligibility for the Child Tax Benefit is established, both the eligible individual and the spouse or common-law partner must file an income tax return each year to maintain eligibility. If the spouse or common-law partner is a non-resident, Form CTB9 must be filed to report their income.

The amounts paid monthly are calculated for a "benefit year"; that is, the period July 1 to June 30. The level of benefits are based on the net family income reported by the parents for the tax year ending before the benefit year.

When the family situation changes, that is the parent marries, starts living common law, separates or divorces, CRA should be notified as soon as possible so that the correct family net income can be taken into account in the calculation of the next child tax benefit amount. Use form RC65 to notify CRA of such changes in marital status.

The Child Tax Benefit has several lucrative components you may qualify to receive for your family:

- *The National Child Tax Benefit.* This consists of a basic amount, a supplement for dependants who are under age 7 in the month plus an additional amount for the third and subsequent dependants. The supplement for children under 7 is reduced by 25% of any child care expenses claimed for the child.

- *The National Child Tax Benefit Supplement.* This is a separate payment for the first child, the second child, and for the third and subsequent children. The annual amount is reduced by a different percentage of the family net income in excess of a base amount, depending on the number of dependants.

- *The Canada Learning Bond.* This is a new notional account which will be payable to parents of children born after 2003 who are eligible for the National Child Tax Benefit Supplement. It allows for an enhanced Canada Education Savings Grant for low income earners who invest money in an RESP for their child. See Chapter 3 for more information.

- *The Child Disability Benefit.* This special amount was announced in the February 2003 Budget. It is paid for each qualified dependant who is eligible for the disability amount.

The Child Tax Benefit is one of the most lucrative provisions in the Income Tax Act for Canadian children. Be sure you maximize it by keeping an eagle eye on the size of your net income (try to keep it below income-testing thresholds with an RRSP deposit. See *Essential Tax Fact Sheets* at www.knowledgebureau.com for income details)

The Goods and Services Tax Credit. Similar to the CTB, the GSTC is not considered to be income to the recipient. Rather it is a way to reimburse low earners, who must pay the Goods and Services Tax, which is based on consumption rather than ability to pay.

The GST/HST Credit is paid quarterly to eligible individuals in respect of themselves, their spouses or common-law partners and qualified dependants. It is based on the family income reported on the income tax return for the year ending before the July 1 benefit year. Note that if the taxpayer has a balance due to CRA, the GST/HST credit may be applied to such outstanding taxes.

Essential TAX FACT #204

If the total GSTC for the year exceeds $100.00 then one-quarter of the amount will be paid in July, October, January, and April. If the total credit is $100 or less, it is paid in July.

Who is eligible to receive it? This is someone who in a particular payment quarter:

Essential TAX FACT #205

Because an individual will become eligible in the quarter following the 19th birthday, it is important that 18-year olds file an income tax return.

Essential TAX FACT #206

Individuals who become residents of Canada in the year should file Form RC151 to apply for the GST/HST Credit. The credit will be paid starting the quarter after the individual becomes a Canadian resident.

Essential TAX FACT #207

If the marital status of an eligible individual changes, CRA should be notified either by letter or using form RC65.

Essential TAX FACT #208

If a qualified individual does not have a cohabiting spouse or common-law partner but does have at least one qualified dependant, an additional amount is payable under the GSTC.

• is at least 19 years old at the beginning of the quarter,

• was a parent who resided with their child, or

• was in a marriage or common-law partnership.

Where two eligible individuals are cohabiting spouses or common-law partners then only one of the eligible individuals may apply for the GST/HST Credit.

A qualified dependant for these purposes is a person who:

• is the child of the individual or dependant for support on the individual or the individual's spouse or common-law partner

• resides with the individual

• is under 19 year of age

The following individuals will not receive the GSTC:

• Deceased individuals

• Persons confined to a prison for at least 90 days which includes the first day of the quarter

• Persons for whom a special allowance under the *Children's Special Allowances Act* is paid

• Non-residents, except those who are married or living common law with a resident of Canada or who were a resident before the quarter

To apply for the Goods and Services/ Harmonized Sales Tax Credit, mark the box labeled "Yes" next to the question "Are you applying for the GST/HST credit?" on page 1 of the T1 return.

See Essential Tax Fact Sheets at www.knowledgebureau.com for more information.

A Special Non-Refundable Tax Credit for Single Parents. Singles should also be interested in a particular non-refundable tax credit available if there is a child in the family. This is known as the Amount for Eligible Dependant and it brings an "equivalent to spouse amount" into the family, based on the dependant's net income.

The credit is found first on Schedule 5 and then is transferred to Schedule 1 of the tax return, line 305. It is available to a taxpayer who:

- did not claim the spouse or common-law partner amount
- was not married or living common law or
- was married or living common law but
  – did not live with a spouse or common-law partner and
  – did not support or was not supported by a spouse or common-law partner

and who supports and lives with a dependant in a home which he or she maintains. To qualify, the dependant must be:

- a child of the taxpayer,
- the taxpayer's parent or grandparent or
- under 18 years of age or wholly dependent on the taxpayer because of mental or physical infirmity.

These qualifications need not be met throughout the year but must be met at some time during the year. In addition the following rules must be observed:

1. Only one person can claim the amount for an eligible dependant in respect of the same dependant.

2. No one may claim the amount for an eligible dependant if someone else is claiming the amount for spouse or common-law partner for that dependant.

3. Only one claim may be made for the amount for an eligible dependant for the same home. Where more than one taxpayer qualifies to make the claim, the taxpayers must agree who will make the claim or no one will be allowed to.

4. If a claim for the amount for an eligible dependant is made in respect of a dependant, no one may claim the amount for infirm dependants or the caregiver amount in respect of the same dependant.

Child Care: A Special Tax Deduction for Working Parents. When you have a child, it is quite likely you may at some point have to pay child care expenses while you work or go to school. Eligible expenses will be claimed as a deduction on the tax return and will reduce your net income—which in turn can increase the refundable tax credits we discussed above. Please see *Essential Tax Fact Sheets* at www.knowledgebureau.com for details of the child care expense claim.

Suddenly single again: planning tax-wise exits

When spouses or common-law partners have lived apart for a period of at least 90 days because of a breakdown of their conjugal relationship, then commencing at the beginning of that 90-day period they will no longer be deemed to be living as spouses.

In the year of such relationship breakdowns, there are numerous significant tax rules to observe including:

- the division of assets,
- spousal or common-law partner RRSPs
- the claiming of child care expenses
- support payments made and received,
- legal fees paid
- federal non-refundable and refundable credits and
- provincial credits.

Essential TAX FACT #209

The Income Tax Act allows for a tax-free rollover of capital assets from a taxpayer to the former spouse on breakdown of the marriage.

Division of Assets. Upon the breakdown of a marriage or common-law relationship, where the terms of a separation or divorce agreement require that the funds from one spouse's DPSP, RESP, RPP, RRSP, or RRIF be transferred to the other, the funds may be transferred on a tax free basis.

Cost of Transferred Property. The transfer of depreciable property takes place at the Undepreciated Capital Cost of the property. As a result, no recapture, terminal loss, or capital gain or loss is incurred on the transfer. For other assets, the transfer takes place at the Adjusted Cost Base of the assets.

Attribution Rules. When one spouse transfers assets to the other, the Attribution Rules generally attribute any income earned by the transferred assets back to the transferor. However the attribution rules do not apply to income earned during the period when the former spouses are living apart because of a breakdown in the relationship.

Spousal RRSPs. Withdrawals from spousal or common-law partner RRSPs made by the annuitant are generally reportable by the contributing spouse if any RRSP contribution has been made in the current year or the previous two years. However, this rule is waived for separated/divorced couples.

Child care expenses. Child care expenses must normally be claimed by the lower income spouse but may be claimed by the higher income spouse during a period where the taxpayer was separated from the other supporting person due to a breakdown in their relationship for a period of at least 90 days as long as they were reconciled within the first 60 days after the taxation year. If the taxpayers were not reconciled within 60 days after the taxation year, then each spouse may claim any child care expenses they paid during the year with no adjustment for child care expenses claimed by the other taxpayer.

Essential TAX FACT #210

Upon relationship breakdown, spouses may elect that gains or losses realized on the disposition of capital property while the taxpayers are living apart should not be allocated back to the other spouse or common-law partner.

Essential TAX FACT #211

The minimum holding requirement is not observed on spousal RRSPs when the taxpayers are living apart as a result of a breakdown in their relationship.

Essential TAX FACT #212

Alimony or support payments made to a spouse or common law partner are taxable to the recipient and deductible by the payor. In the year of separation or divorce, however, the payer may claim either the deduction for support of the spousal amount, but not both.

Legal Fees on Separation or Divorce. Legal fees to obtain a divorce or separation agreement are normally not deductible. However, as of October 10, 2002, CRA considers legal costs incurred to obtain spousal support relating specifically to the care of children (not the spouse) under the Divorce Act or under provincial legislation in a separation agreement, as well as the costs incurred to obtain an increase in support or make child support non-taxable will be deductible.

Federal Refundable Tax Credits. The Child Tax Benefit (CTB) and Goods and Services Tax Credit (GSTC) are forward-looking amounts. That is, they are received as a redistribution of income for the purpose of assistance with the current expenses of mid and low income earners in the next "benefit year"—July to June. But, they are calculated based on net family income from the prior tax year.

Essential TAX FACT #213

When a family break-down occurs, CRA should be immediately notified so that the calculation of the credits for the next CTB or GSTC payment may be made without including the estranged spouse or common-law partner's net income.

Immediate notification of change in marital sttus is most important to supplement monthly income, especially in the case of the CTB. Also, be sure to do so because the statute of limitations for recovery of missed or underpaid credits is generally only 11 months, although some leniency may be applied here.

The Income Tax Act assumes that the eligible CTB recipient is the female parent, however, "prescribed factors" will be considered in determining what constitutes care and upbringing and who is fulfilling that responsibility.

For example, where, after the breakdown of a conjugal relationship, the single parent and child returns to live with his or her parents, the single parent will continue to be presumed to be the supporting individual unless they too are under 18 years old. In that case, the grandparents may claim the Child Tax Benefit for both their child and their grandchild.

Provincial Tax Credits. Many provinces have tax reductions or refundable credits that are based on family net income. In most cases, in the year of separation, it is not necessary to include the estranged spouse or common-law partner's income in the family income calculation and normally no credits or reductions on behalf of the estranged spouse or common-law partner will be allowed. Each partner will claim the credits or reductions to which he or she is entitled.

Singles who give care to dependant adults

It is possible to be single and give care, either alone, or in conjunction with other caregivers. For example, two single siblings could be sharing the care of an aging, disabled parent together. In that case, the Income Tax Act allows for the splitting of certain non-refundable tax credits. The significant credits you should be familiar with are:

Amount for Eligible Dependants. As discussed under Single Parents, taxpayers who do not have a spouse or common-law partner but who maintained a dwelling in Canada and supported a person related by blood, marriage or adoption who was under 18 and lived with them in that dwelling may claim the Amount for an Eligible Dependant (formally know as the Equivalent-to-Spouse amount). The Amount for Eligible Dependants is reduced by dependant's Net Income in excess of certain maximums. (See *Essential Tax Fact Sheets* at www.knowledge-bureau.com for recent figures.) Only one claim may be made for each dwelling and for each dependant. Singles and other supporting individuals may also qualify to claim:

Essential TAX FACT #214

If you are single, you may wish to claim an Amount for Eligible Dependant or the Caregiver Amount, whichever yields a better overall result. Claims can be split between caregivers, provided that the total amount claimed for the same dependant does not exceed one full claim.

Amount of Infirm Dependants 18 and Over. If you support a dependant who is 18 and over and mentally or physically infirm, a special credit is available, based on that dependant's net income level. This will include income from Old Age Security Supplements, Guaranteed Income Supplements, Spouse's Allowances, CPP benefits, EI Benefits, Worker's Compensation Payments and Social Assistance. Members of your extended family may qualify—parents, grandparents, siblings,

Essential TAX FACT #215

The Caregiver Amount will not be claimable unless the dependant is living with you— even if you provide substantially all supports to your dependant in their home.

aunts, uncles, nephews, nieces, and in-laws—all may qualify if infirm and living in Canada.

Caregiver Amount. If you care for an elderly parent or grandparent or other disabled dependant who is over 18 years old and living with you in your home, you may be eligible to claim the Caregiver Amount. This claim is also based on the dependant's net income, but is phased out at higher income threshold levels, making it possible to arrive at a claim even if the dependant is receiving Old Age Security and Canada Pension Plan income. If a claim for an Amount for an Eligible Dependant was also made for this dependant, the Caregiver Amount will also be reduced by that claim.

Essential TAX FACT #216

To qualify for the Disability Amount, the taxpayer must suffer from a severe and prolonged ailment that is expected to last for a continuous period of at least twelve months.

Disability Amount. This is possibly one of the most lucrative, yet most missed provisions on the tax return. It requires the signing of a form by a medical practitioner—*Form T2201 Disability Tax Credit Certificate.*

This means that if a person was diagnosed with cancer in September and the condition of the disease became debilitating by the end of the year, the amount would be claimable for the whole year.

The condition must "markedly restrict" the patient. Examples are:

- Blindness at any time in the year

- Inability to feed or dress oneself (or situations in which this is possible but only after taking an inordinately long period of time to do so)

- Inability to perform basic functions, even with therapy or the use of devices and medication. These can include:
  – Perceiving, thinking, remembering or other cognitive functions
  – Speaking to be understood by a familiar person in a quiet setting
  – Hearing to understand a familiar person in a quiet setting
  – Walking
  – Controlling bowel and/or bladder functions

In addition, those persons who receive therapy to support a vital function—like kidney dialysis for an average of at least 14 hours a week, will qualify to claim this credit. A supplement is available for those who support disabled children. However, if child care expenses are claimed for the child, the supplement will be reduced.

If the amount is not needed by the disabled person because that person is not taxable, the amount can be transferred to a supporting individual. If that person is a spouse, use Schedule 2; otherwise a special line is allocated for transfers from other dependants: Line 318. There are some special rules in making this claim to take note of, however:

- The Disability Amount and the Disability Supports Deduction may both be claimed on the tax return, however, that deduction could limit the disability amount supplement claimed for minor children

- The taxpayer cannot claim both the costs of nursing home care or full time attendant care as a medical expense, together with the Disability Amount. One or the other can be claimed but not both.

- Those who pay someone to come into the home to provide care for the sick may claim expenditures up to $10,000 ($20,000 in the year of death) and then still claim the Disability Amount.

New rules for claiming medical expenses

The claim for medical expenses is one of the most common provisions on the return—it affects the majority of tax filers—yet it is most often under-claimed and misunderstood.

Medical expenses may be claimed for:

- the taxpayer, the taxpayer's spouse or common-law partner;

- a child or grandchild of the taxpayer or the taxpayer's spouse who depended on the taxpayer for support, and

Essential TAX FACT #217

Medical expenses can be claimed for the best 12-month period ending in the tax year. To do so, medical expenses should be grouped within a twelve month period that bears the best claim. This could be February 1, to January 31, May 1 to April 30 and so on.

Essential TAX FACT #218

In the year of death, the normal 12-month period for making the medical expense claim is increased to a 24-month period that includes the date of death. Medical expenses by the executor paid after death may be claimed.

Essential TAX FACT #219

Starting in 2004 medical expenses for dependant adults may be added to the return of a supporting individual, but that claim is calculated separately on Line 331 of the return. Total medical expenses must be reduced by 3% of the dependant's net income and the maximum claim under this category is $5,000 in '04; $10,000 in '05, applied separately to each individual claimed here and the claim must be for the same 12 month period chosen for medical expenses made at Line 330.

Essential TAX FACT #220

As long as the taxpayer is a resident of Canada, medical expenses incurred abroad are also claimable, including Blue Cross and other travel or private health insurance premiums.

Essential TAX FACT #221

The taxpayer may claim travel expenses for the patient and one attendant who must travel 80 km or more to receive medical services not available in their community.

• under special new rules, adult children or grandchildren, a parent, grandparent, brother, sister, uncle, aunt, niece, or nephew of the taxpayer or the taxpayer's spouse who lived in Canada at any time in the year and depended on the taxpayer for support.

In the case of expenditures for the first three groups of dependants, the total claim for medical expenses are co-mingled and then reduced by 3% of the taxpayer's net income. The claim is made at Line 330 of the tax return. It may be to your advantage to claim the medical expenses on the return of the lower-income taxpayer, because of this limitation, unless that taxpayer is not taxable.

Allowable medical expenditures. See *Essential Tax Fact Sheets* at www.knowledgebureau.com for a list of allowable payments to medical practitioners, or for treatments and devices.

Blue Cross and similar private health insurance premiums are often deducted by the employer; the amount paid by the employer and included in the employee's income will be shown on the T4 slip; amounts paid by the employee will likely be shown on pay stubs.

Note, when travelling to receive medical services, actual receipts can be used for costs of travel including gas, hotel and meals, or you can claim vehicle expenses using a simplified method based on a rate per kilometre. This method does not require receipts to be kept for vehicle expenses, only a record of the number of kilometres driven. If you are travelling from B.C. to Alberta for treatment, the rate is calculated based on the province in which the trip began (B.C. in this case). For ongoing current rates, visit the CRA web site.

Essential TAX FACT #222

Wealth can be effectively passed along to others during your lifetime or upon your demise. But what's important is that you begin immediately to set up an estate plan with your financial advisors and that you have a will.

Preparing for death and widowhood

No personal financial plan can be completed without a plan for transferring assets to the next generation, yet the majority of Canadians are reluctant to discuss the transfer of their assets with family members and many don't have a will. But to paraphrase Benjamin Franklin, death and taxes are perhaps the only two constants we can count on from the moment of birth… and it pays well to be prepared for the inevitable.

A lifetime of complicated personal relationships makes that more difficult, especially if you are wealthy. Whether you are already alone, or preparing to be alone, protecting your assets at the time of death is an important obligation to your family as well as society. Consider the following checklist for starting an estate plan:

OBJECTIVES FOR STARTING AN ESTATE PLAN

- *Identify Financial Institutions*: where are your assets held? Include key contacts.
- *Identify Advisors*: Who are your professional advisors including banker, accountant, lawyer, stockbroker, insurance agent and what is their contact info?
- *Identify Proxies*: Who will exercise Power of Attorney if you become disable; or cannot direct your own personal health or financial affairs?
- *Identify Heirs*: list exact contact information, as well as their relationship to you. In the case of singles, these heirs could include your

favorite charity. Discuss options for transfer of assets and funds during your lifetime and at death.

- *Identify Gifts*: sketch out what you wish for each of your heirs to receive.

- *Identify Needs*: will any of your heirs require assistance with ongoing income?

- *Identify Executors*: prepare a list of possible executor(s) and make approaches.

- *Identify Guardians*: prepare a list of those to whom you would trust the care of your minor children, as well those who should not have that responsibility.

- *Identify Business Succession Plans*: How should your business interests be distributed, and who should step in to run the show?

- *Plan for probate fees and capital gains taxes at death.* Review life insurance policies that may be used for those purposes.

- *Identify Capital Assets* and their fair market value annually.

- *Identify Asset Transfer Instructions*: which assets should be transferred during your lifetime, and which should be transferred only upon your death?

- *Make Plans for Safekeeping.* Keep all important documents in a safety deposit box and identify the location.

- *Deal with Debt.* Cleaning up spilled milk is no fun for anyone. . .especially if it's been there for awhile. List debt obligations and the order they should be repaid. Make a list of on-going financial obligations that should be cancelled upon death.

- *Draw up your will.* Tell your lawyer where it is to be kept.

Charitable Donations. Most Canadians give to charities at some point in the year. Those gifts, usually of money, will be claimed on the tax return, first on *Schedule 9 Donations and Gifts,* and then on Schedule 1. The amounts donated to Registered Canadian Charities must be supported by receipts that have official registration numbers.

The claim for donations is a two-tiered federal credit: 16% on the first $200 and 29% on the balance. The real dollar value is higher than this, when provincial taxes are factored in. Therefore it may be advantageous to group donations between spouses, or common law partners who are allowed to act as agents for each other and claim each other's donations, or, in the case of singles, to carry forward donations for up to five years, for a better claim.

Filing Consequences at time of death. When you die, one mandatory final return must filed for the period January 1 to date of death, and this return must be done by the later of:

- April 30 of the year immediately following the year of death

- six months after date of death

However, the final return from January to date of death is usually the only one most taxpayers will file. On that return, income earned up to date of death is reported. This will

Essential TAX FACT #226

A special tax break is allowed when publicly traded mutual funds, shares, stock options, bonds, bills, warrants or futures listed on a prescribed stock exchange are donated to charity: the income inclusion on disposition of these assets will be one half the normal capital gains inclusion rates. Complete, *Form T1170 Capital Gains on Gifts of Certain Capital Property.*

Essential TAX FACT #227

A transfer of shares of a private Canadian Controlled Corporation to a charity is ignored at the time of the donation; with the donations credit being claimed if the security is disposed of within five years. This includes disposition by death of donor; however, the donations credit will be allowed at that time if the donor dies before the five-year period is up.

Essential TAX FACT #228

There are several "elective returns" that can be filed as well, which will allow you to claim again certain personal amounts, to result in a substantial tax benefit.

Essential TAX FACT #229

The most significant transaction on the final return could revolve around the disposition of capital assets. That's because a deemed disposition of your assets is considered to have taken place at date of death.

Essential TAX FACT #230

If you transfer capital property to your spouse during your lifetime, resulting capital gains or losses on disposition are taxed back in your hands, unless a bona fide loan is drawn up, as discussed in earlier chapters. In general, no disposition will be considered to have taken place at fair market value at that time, unless you so elect.

Essential TAX FACT #231

Be sure to provide your executor a copy of the 1994 tax return and in particular Form T664 upon which a capital gains election may have been made to use up the taxpayer's $100,000 Capital Gains Exemption. This will affect the calculation of the deemed disposition of capital properties on the final return.

mean that certain income sources must be "prorated" to date of death, for example, employment earnings, pension receipts, interest, dividend, rents, royalties, or annuity income accrued. Offsetting expenses are accrued to date of death in a similar fashion.

When you die, you are deemed to have disposed of your assets immediately before death, usually at Fair Market Value (FMV), however, the value of the deemed disposition can vary, dpending on who will acquire the assets. . .your spouse (including common-law partner), child or another. Transfers to children or others are generally made at the property's FMV; transfers to spouse can be at the asset's adjusted cost base (or UCC in the case of depreciable assets) or FMV.

The use of "tax free rollovers". The deemed disposition rules upon death of the taxpayer therefore override the Attribution Rules in existence while living. That is, capital property transferred to the spouse upon your death will not be taxed until that spouse disposes of the property. The spouse will use your adjusted cost base, and pay tax on the full gain from the time you acquired the asset, thereby completely avoiding tax consequences at the time of your death.

Depending on your taxable income status at the time of your death, your executor may wish to rollover assets to the spouse on a tax free basis, or choose fair market value. This may make sense if you have unused capital loss balances from the past, that have been carried forward. Such balances can often be used to offset income created by the higher valuations. It will also provide your survivors with the opportunity to record higher adjusted cost base figures upon acquisition of your assets, which will save them money down the line as well.

In the absence of those deliberate plans, capital gains or losses resulting from the deemed disposition of the deceased's assets must be reported, together with any recapture or terminal loss on depreciable assets, with the resulting tax payable (if any) on that return.

Essential TAX FACT #232

Request a clearance certificate from CRA to absolve the executor of any further liability.

RRSPs and Other Pensions. Didn't spend it all? What happens when you die and leave unspent accumulations in your RRSP?

Essential TAX FACT #233

Try not to make major financial or lifestyle changes within one year after the death of a spouse.

A taxpayer is deemed to have received the fair market value of all assets in his RRSP or RRIF immediately prior to death. If there is a surviving spouse or common-law partner then the assets may be transferred tax-free to that person. Similar provisions allow for the transfer of Deferred Profit Sharing Plans, Registered Pension Plan Benefits, and Registered Retirement Income Funds (RRIF) assets. In certain circumstances, the RRSP can be transferred to a financially dependent child or grandchild, even when there is a surviving spouse. Speak to your tax advisors about these options.

CHAPTER SUMMATION:

ESSENTIAL TAX FACTS FOR SINGLES AND SENIORS

Special tax provisions are available for junior and senior singles who are humming along just fine on their own, or providing loving care and support to dependants around them. Modern lifestyles and demographic challenges drive tax change, and so it is important for you to be aware and make the tax system work for you in whatever lifecycle you find yourself in. Ask your tax and financial advisors about the tax provisions available:

For Those Who Live Alone
- Maximization of income diversification and deferral options
- Creation of tax exempt, as well as tax efficient asset holdings
- Retirement income planning strategies in the absence of income splitting opportunities
- Maximization of tax deductible spousal support and legal fees
- Charitable donation strategies for estate planning
- Maximization of non-refundable credits:
  - overpayments of source deductions for CPP and EI
  - the age amount (for those age 65 and older)
  - the pension income amount (for those who receive private pension income)
  - the disability amount
  - medical expenses
- Maximization of refundable tax credits:
  - the GSTC as well as provincial tax credits
  - medical expenses supplement (only if there is earned income from employment of self-employment).

For Those Who Care for a Spouse or Common-Law Partner or former partner
- Consider conjugal or marital status if reconciliation takes place
- If providing care to a sick spouse or common-law partner, be sure to consider claiming:
  - an increased spousal amount
  - transfer of the spouse's age, disability, pension or tuition and education amounts
  - the claiming of medical expenses and charitable donations
  - the claiming of the medical expense supplement — but only if there is income from employment or self-employment sources.

For single parents, in addition to some of the provisions above

- reporting of taxable support payments and requirement to make instalment payments
- Use of RRSP deduction to increase refundable and non-refundable tax credits
- child care expenses
- amount for eligible dependant
- refundable tax credits; in particular the Child Tax Benefit
- RESP deposits

For Those Who Care for Other Relatives

If you are providing care to other relatives who are sick, your advisor will be claiming the following credits and asking you for supporting documents:

- the amount for infirm dependants age 18 and older
- the caregiver amount
- the claiming of medical expenses for that dependant.

NOW PUT MORE MONEY IN YOUR POCKET ALL YEAR LONG...

PERSPECTIVE

We hope that we have accomplished our mission in writing this book: to show you hundreds of simple ways to put more money in your pocket at tax time—and all year long. We hope that you will be motivated to take control of your after-tax results and learn even more. The checklist that follows might help you develop a script to start this discussion with your professional financial advisors:

Essential TAX FACT #234	
Set goals and objectives: for short and long term personal financial plans.	

- Review personal financial statements: net worth, cash flow, budget, bank reconciliation, balance sheets and income and expense statements.
- Take stock of RRSP Contribution Room: contribute to your RRSP regularly.
- Acquire a tax-exempt personal residence.
- Maximize earnings from non-registered savings: by keeepinf an eagle eye on after-tax returns.
- Accumulate capital.
- Choose your mate with care. Mistakes here can really set you back. Plan the end of your relationship while you still like each other.
- Be ready for family. Be emotionally and financially secure enough to do a great job raising your children. Don't let them down—they are the future.
- Have the right kind of insurance: Protect yourself, your family and your business from calamities beyond your control.
- Have a will. No matter how young you are, plan for your demise along the way to capture the full power of your productivity. Update annually at tax filing time.
- Stay current: Keep on top of the changing tax rules throughout your lifetime.
- Be aware of lifecycle change. Revisit your goals during times of change.
- Embrace lifelong learning: seek educational opportunities that result in new thinking, analytical skills as well as "hands on" experiences.
- But… you can't know everything: enlist the help of a professional team dedicated to your goals.

Essential TAX FACT #235

Managing your money will be a lifelong affair. Keeping on top of your right to arrange your affairs within the framework of the law to pay only the correct amount of tax—and not one cent more—will enhance the process. But, in the end, remember that your money is only a tool that will help you in your quest for self-actualization.

INDEX